on track ...
Korn

every album, every song

Matt Karpe

sonicbondpublishing.com

Sonicbond Publishing Limited
www.sonicbondpublishing.co.uk
Email: info@sonicbondpublishing.co.uk

First Published in the United Kingdom 2021
First Published in the United States 2021

British Library Cataloguing in Publication Data:
A Catalogue record for this book is available from the British Library

Copyright Matt Karpe 2021

ISBN 978-1-78952-153-5

Typeset in ITC Garamond & ITC Avant Garde
Printed and bound in England

Graphic design and typesetting: Full Moon Media

on track ...
Korn
every album, every song

Matt Karpe

sonicbondpublishing.com

Acknowledgements

Thank you to Stephen Lambe for the trust and taking on this book.

Thank you to my parents for their continued support.

Thank you to my fiancée, Carly, for believing in me and always encouraging me to follow my dreams.

Most importantly – thank you to Jonathan Davis, Brian Welch, James Shaffer, Regi Arvizu, David Silveria and Ray Luzier for creating such incredible music over the last three decades.

on track ...

Korn

Contents

Introduction

Bakersfield, a charter city in Kern County, California, is some three hours from Los Angeles. Yet in itself, it is a thriving location known for its music culture covering a variety of styles and genres.

The Bakersfield Symphony Orchestra has been performing classical music for well over 80 years; the city's very own Merle Haggard produced his own form of country music, which would later earn the term 'The Bakersfield Sound', while Doo-wop rhythm and blues from the 1950s and 1960s also put the city on the music map. And then there is heavy metal and Bakersfield's favourite sons, a band who many years later would have 24 February officially declared 'Korn Day' by their hometown mayor, and even have their own road named after them (Korn Row).

In the late 1980s, a funk metal band by the name of L.A.P.D. was hitting its stride with three parts of the line-up featuring the then-unknown Reginald 'Fieldy' Arvizu on bass (his nickname shortened from the original Garfield – because he had big cheeks), who, although he was left-handed, played bass with his right, James 'Munky' Shaffer on guitar (his nickname given by Arvizu as his feet supposedly looked like monkey hands), who only started to learn the guitar as a form of rehabilitation after severing the tip of his left index finger on a bike chain, and David (just David) Silveria on drums. Feeling that the bright lights of Los Angeles would give themselves a better chance of succeeding, where the likes of Mötley Crüe and Guns N' Roses were proving the city's music value was just as important as its Hollywood movie empire, L.A.P.D. relocated to Huntington Beach. Just a stone's throw from downtown L.A., the band released their debut EP, *Love and Peace Dude*, in 1989 via Triple X Records, and then a first full-length album in 1991 titled *Who's Laughing Now*. At this time, a friend of theirs by the name of Brian 'Head' Welch (his nickname coming from the fact he thought he had a big head), was filling in as a second guitarist and also acting as the band's roadie during live shows, but when the band upped sticks, he decided to remain in Bakersfield and travel to L.A. when he was needed.

Back in Bakersfield, a band called SexArt was starting to earn a name for themselves with their brash form of alternative metal, and amongst their ranks was a weedy new romantic by the name of Jonathan Davis. Working in a mortuary by day and trying to figure out how to be a heavy metal frontman by night, Davis battled self-doubt in the beginning. 'I had no clue what I was doing', he was quoted as saying in Leah Furman's 2000 book, *Korn: Life in the Pit*, 'I didn't even know what the hell to do with my voice.'

Over in Huntington Beach, L.A.P.D. had left Triple X after being given an ultimatum to clean up their act. Despite selling enough copies of their *Who's Laughing Now* album to be able to tour the US and Europe, and having earned a strong following through two years of relentless gigging, the band had become notorious for their mischievous behaviour, which included causing damage to backstage areas, throwing food, and urinating in the dip. Making it hard for Triple X to keep throwing money their way and having been banned from many venues in Los Angeles, L.A.P.D. felt it unfair to be called out by their record label, so the two decided to go their separate ways. Later calling it quits altogether after their vocalist Richard Morral up and left, Shaffer, Arvizu and Silveria formed a new band called Creep. Hiring Welch as an official second guitarist, all Creep required now was a larger-than-life frontman to give them an edge over their contemporaries. While Shaffer and Welch visited family in Bakersfield, they went to a show which included SexArt on the bill, and upon witnessing Jonathan Davis in action, Creep attempted to take him back to Huntington Beach to complete the missing piece of their puzzle.

Appreciative of the offer but initially hesitant to accept, Davis reportedly visited a psychic who advised the singer it would be beneficial to move to L.A. and join Creep. Seeing that as the sign he needed to take a risk, Davis went and auditioned for the band, got the gig, and within two weeks, Korn was born. Interviewed years later by Rolling Stone, Davis looked back on his decision to leave Bakersfield: 'I had to fucking quit my day job where I was making great money as a mortician, I had my own house, to fucking having nothing and working at a pizza place as a shift manager living under some stairs.'

Deciding on their band name after Davis had heard a disgusting story told by some of his gay friends (we'll leave it at that), the five-piece chose to spell their name with a 'K' instead of a 'C' and use a backwards 'R'- the idea of that coming from the Toys R Us logo which, incidentally, was a store where various members of the band had worked previously. Renting the Underground Chicken Sound studio in Huntington Beach, the band would create weird and whacky heavy music, unlike anything that was around at the time and, before long, crowds of people would congregate outside of the studio to try to fuel their intrigue by seeing and hearing what was going on. 'It'd be us doing odd jobs, just trying to hustle money to scrape beer money together and still have rehearsal money,' said Shaffer in a 2016 interview with *Metal Hammer*. 'We tried to get money in whatever ways we could- washing cars, moving furniture- and then maybe we'd go to the beach and surf a little, and party all night.'

By the summer of 1993, Korn had started playing shows and building a fanbase, and it is there that we join the band's road to superstardom – with a hell of a lot of brilliant music, chaos and self-destruction along the way. Fasten your seatbelts.

Neidermayer's Mind (1993)

Personnel:
Jonathan Davis: vocals
Brian 'Head' Welch: guitar
James 'Munky' Shaffer: guitar
Reginald 'Fieldy' Arvizu: bass guitar
David Silveria: drums
Record label: self-released
Recorded at: Underground Chicken Sound Studios, 1993
Produced by: Ross Robinson
Release date: 17 October 1993
Highest chart positions: N/A
Running time: 17:55

Joining up with then-unknown producer Ross Robinson, Korn created their first demo tape and released it in limited quantities in October 1993. Sent out to record labels and also to people who filled out a flyer the band gave out at Biohazard and House of Pain shows, where Korn played for free – *Neidermayer's Mind* wasn't particularly well-received by the public nor music critics. It is also worth noting that the tape was released without an official title, but it became known through the correlation with the artist who designed its cover art, and so the *Neidermayer's Mind* moniker was adopted by fans.

Perhaps due to the band themselves rather than their demo, Korn did manage to catch the attention of someone, and that someone was Paul Pontius – an Immortal Records A&R who would describe the band's sound as 'the new genre of rock'; and he wasn't wrong. More for purists, *Neidermayer's Mind* is still worth a listen from time to time. While Korn was still figuring out their path to global domination, there are still moments across the four tracks which hint at their musical capabilities even at such a green age. Unsurprisingly, it is raw and rough around the edges – but what demo tapes aren't?

Original pressings remain highly sought after, and if you want one, you are going to have to search far and wide. Every so often, one pops up online, but you will need to make sure you have plenty of money to entice someone into selling it. Bootlegs have also been released over the years, but they are just as hard to come by, and there is always YouTube, where the original recordings are readily available to investigate at the click of a button.

'Predictable' (Korn)

People's first experience of hearing Korn came on this grungy number, and before you shout 'typo!', 'Predictable' is exactly how the band spelt it and released it. Jonathan Davis is yet to find his true voice as he sings with a Scott Weiland/Axl Rose snarl on these recordings, but there are moments where the listener sits up and takes notice of a different type of frontman. Instrumentally, the band sounds extremely cohesive, and although a reworked version would

11

feature on Korn's debut album (and spelt correctly too), this raw and groovy rendition is arguably better the first time around.

'Blind' (Korn, Dennis Shinn)
A year from now, it would become one of the most ground-breaking songs of the 1990s, but this version of 'Blind' also has a certain magic to it. Generally following the formula of that which was penned by Dennis Shinn from the SexArt days, a quicker intro full of extended thick instrumentation really shows Korn's vision for the first time. Riff-heavy and with a more urgent tempo, 'Blind' reeks of star quality long before anyone would truly take notice of the quintet.

'Daddy' (Korn, Dennis Shinn)
Another song that would be turned into a whole new monster in twelve month's time, the demo version of 'Daddy' is shorter in length and contains a different chorus to that which would close out Korn's debut album. Regi Arvizu's bass riff opens proceedings, and while Davis sings with shaky commitment, you get the feeling that he is still singing someone else's song as, once again, Dennis Shinn wrote the original version before Korn would make it into their own. Different and appealing, this 'Daddy' demo doesn't have the same impact and shock value of what it would soon spawn into, but perhaps that is a good thing as Korn's main aim in 1993 was to lay down some early foundations.

'Alive' (Korn)
It would be over a decade before a polished version of 'Alive' would be made available to hear, featuring on Korn's sixth studio album, *Take a Look in the Mirror*. Containing a Pantera-like metal thump with crunching riffs and fast and frantic drum sections, Davis lets Welch take on the lead vocal role on this one and his feisty snarl fits with the brash soundscape on show. Korn originally scrapped 'Alive' and worked some of its sections into their 1994 track, 'Need To'; however, this is another song that showed small glimpses of the potential Korn had at their very early disposal.

Korn (1994)

Personnel:
Jonathan Davis: vocals, bagpipes
Brian 'Head' Welch: guitar
James 'Munky' Shaffer: guitar
Reginald 'Fieldy' Arvizu: bass guitar
David Silveria: drums
Record label: Immortal, Epic
Recorded at: Indigo Ranch Studios, Malibu, California, USA, May-June 1994
Produced by: Ross Robinson
Release date: 11 October 1994
Highest chart positions: US: 72, UK: 181
Running time: 65:45

Honestly, when we were labelled the band that invented the style of ... what
do they call it, 'Nu rock'? I guess people say we invented this nu metal sound
or whatever. I never really thought of it like that. I just thought we were doing
our thing. That's just what came natural from all our influences as musicians. I
never really thought, 'Hey, we've invented this new kind of music, this is going
to be huge'. (The) Thought never even crossed my mind.
David Silveria quote from an interview with *Rolling Stone*

Heavy metal looked to be in a healthy state in 1994, after riding the wave
of grunge's short burst in the spotlight, which seemingly ended upon Kurt
Cobain's suicide in the first quarter of the year. Pantera, Nine Inch Nails,
Machine Head and Testament all released critically acclaimed albums
throughout 1994; however, the whole heavy metal spectrum would change
forever on 11 October, when Korn announced themselves to an unsuspecting
world.

Sporting Adidas tracksuits, baggy jeans and unkempt dreadlocks, playing
seven-string guitars, primordial in their down-tuned settings, and accompanied
by an assortment of effects pedals, not to mention the funky rattle of the bass
which added to heavy instrumentation more in-keeping with hip-hop than
metal – Korn emerged with a sound unlike anything heard before on their self-
titled debut album.

By now, they had already secured a deal with Immortal Records and a
distribution deal with Epic Records, all thanks to Paul Pontius, who stumbled
across the band and quickly noticed there was something different about them
compared to the rest of the metal bands floating around at the time. Content
with Ross Robinson's production work on the *Neidermayer's Mind* demo,
Korn once again enlisted his expertise for their first full-length, and as well as
transferring the band's sound to tape, Robinson was able to add the raw and
stark reality of the sub-plots which Korn used as influences to write twelve
unnerving and deeply unsettling songs. Bringing out the darkest pieces of

Jonathan Davis' history in order to obtain the most real and honest performances out of the frontman, Robinson pushed and prodded with unrelenting prowess, which, in the end, would leave Davis a broken shell of a man.

Featuring subject matters of trauma, bullying, addiction and abuse, all relayed through the tortured howls and almost confessional refrains of Davis, Korn's debut album reinvigorated heavy metal whilst also ushering in a new movement which would later go on to be labelled 'Nu Metal'.

Having spent much of their early days experimenting and crafting their sound in the small Huntington Beach house the five band members shared together, as well as holing themselves up in the Underground Chicken Sound studio, evenings saw both locations become the settings for big parties where those in attendance were considered Korn's primary fan base. An abundance of cheap booze and vast quantities of meth were heavily consumed, as Korn acted like rock stars long before they would ever be considered as such.

With the album ready to record, Indigo Ranch in Malibu was the studio of choice, hand-picked by Ross Robinson who later told *Rolling Stone*, 'The reason I picked Indigo Ranch was because Neil Young was there, Neil Diamond, all these really killer old-schoolers. I think Lenny Kravitz was there, and Nick Cave. I knew that recording raw and vintage, the album wouldn't sound dated, ever.' Recorded in a little over a month at a reported cost of no more than $14,000, *Korn* wouldn't necessarily earn its creators any overnight success, instead a slow-burning ascension ensued where touring proved pivotal in bringing the band to people's national (and latterly international) attention.

After a less than successful start to touring life with shows alongside Biohazard and House of Pain, and the death of the band's very first tour bus, which had been paid for by their record label, Korn resumed their expansive promotional campaign at the beginning of 1995 by supporting punk rockers Sick of It All, the goth rocking Danzig (and Marilyn Manson), and thrash metal legends, Megadeth. A first trek over to Europe followed later in the year, the first show of which took place in Nottingham, England, and by this time, four singles had already been released from the album. 'Blind', 'Need To', 'Shoots and Ladders' and 'Clown' were four of the standout songs on Korn, but only 'Blind' charted anywhere (15 on Canada's RPM Alternative 30), while the album itself peaked at 72 on the *Billboard* 200 in America – which, all things considered, wasn't to be sniffed at.

Having played over 200 shows in 1995 where Korn also shared stages with Ozzy Osbourne, Metallica and Life of Agony, the Bakersfield five had greatly enhanced their standing within the heavy metal community, gripping their young adult target audience who were looking for a new kind of music to call their own. With subject matters perhaps relatable to what they were dealing with in their own lives, the songs on *Korn* acted as a kind of remedy to some, who were able to realise that they were not alone in what issues they were dealing with and the emotions that they were feeling.

To further underline Korn's intention to shock and stun, the album's artwork perfectly accompanied the music's dark and atmospheric nature. Depicting a young girl on a swing, shielding the sun from her eyes whilst trying to make out a spooky and shadowy figure standing over her with what looked like claws for hands, the vivid imagery unsurprisingly caused a stir upon its unveiling. The girl – eight-year-old Justine Ferrara – was the niece of Paul Pontius, the man who first discovered Korn. Paid $300 for the photoshoot, the images taken by Stephen Stickler, Justine would not see the finished articles until she was in eighth grade, as her parents were horrified at their daughter's portrayal. Positioning the Korn logo, so the girl's shadow looked like it was hanging from it, the connotations of the cover were further enhanced by the rear artwork, which simply showed an empty swing and no one in sight. Pontius himself may have caused some family division at the time, but it was just another vital aspect in helping Korn – both the band and the album, enter the fray with a complete package to give to anyone who dared check out this intriguing new metal band.

In January 1996, *Korn* was certified gold in America, a year later, it had gone platinum, and by November 1999, it had reached double-platinum status; and with it, five unwitting dudes from Bakersfield had become the pioneers of a new form of heavy metal music.

'Blind' (Korn, Dennis Shinn)

Originally written by Davis' bandmate in SexArt, Dennis Shinn's version was generally what people heard on the *Neidermayer's Mind* demo before Korn took on 'Blind' and turned it into the anthem everyone knows today. 'It was Korn's professionalism that brought the song to life', Shinn was later quoted as saying, and the results were there for all to see in 1994.

Opening with Silveria's ride cymbal being repeatedly struck in double time, Welch and Shaffer then debut with a single chord progression and distorted counter-riff, which builds tension to almost unbearable limits, and then 'Blind' explodes into life with Davis' now-legendary call to arms cry of 'Are you readyyy?!'. Written about the singer's already forceful drug problems (primarily with methamphetamines), 'Blind' contains references to Davis' chaotic life experiences as he explores ways to cope with the effects of his drug use brought on by the trauma he suffered in his younger years. Blistering power and abrasive discipline from the seven-string guitars roar the song forward, while Davis switches between tender and vigorous vocal deliveries to give most people their first experience of hearing him sing. Moody, intense and completely different to what else was coming out back in 1994, a glorious and groove-laden crescendo finds Korn setting their stall out from the get-go with a song now firmly etched in heavy metal folklore.

For many, the promo video for 'Blind' was the first time people had the chance to see the band behind the music, and while the video is a relatively simple affair, the small venue in which Korn perform perfectly captures their raw intensity. Largely shot in black and white and also offering some footage of the band members hanging out in California, it is the performance of 'Blind' which deserves the viewer's full attention. With a large banner hosting Korn's soon-to-be trademark logo, on full show behind David Silveria and his drum kit, a small crowd show their frenzied energy with mosh pits and crowd surfing galore, while Jonathan Davis goes batshit crazy in his Adidas tracksuit and Shaffer and Welch rock some less than trendy boiler suits.

Even watching the video today gives you a feeling of just how important a moment Korn's debut was back in 1994, and *YouTube* perfectly summed it up in a 2020 article when George Garner called the video an 'Epiphanic moment in the history of heavy metal'. With over 66 million views on Korn's YouTube channel, the Joseph 'McG' McGinty Nichol-directed promo remains a ground-breaking moment in nu metal's early inception.

'Ball Tongue' (Korn)

Led by Arvizu's bouncing bass slaps, 'Ball Tongue' continued Korn's early assault with one of the more aggressive and multi-layered songs on the album. Again, musically taking inspiration from 1990s hip-hop, 'Ball Tongue' was written about a friend of the band who liked his meth and helped some of the band members get hooked on it too. In his *Save Me from Myself* memoir released in 2007, Welch had this to say about the man behind the song's story, 'Sometimes he would get so geeked out on speed that he couldn't talk, no matter how hard he tried. He would just sit there with his mouth open, tongue sticking out, and his tongue looked like it had a little ball on the end of it.'

Featuring Davis' schizophrenic vocal stylings, his frenzied barking and belligerent growls were in part due to being high on meth at the time of recording. Offering an early glimpse of his scat vocal, which would become famous on later tracks of future albums, 'Ball Tongue' proved the band wasn't a one-trick pony as a colossal bout of instrumentation plays out with the inclusion of beer kegs being repeatedly whacked. For those still catching their breath after 'Blind', 'Ball Tongue' offered very little respite.

'Need To' (Korn)

Featuring elements of the 'Alive' demo from *Neidermayer's Mind*, 'Need To' is dominated by Arvizu's bass work and Silveria's pounding drum sections. Murky and with a hint of grunge filtering through, one of the more accessible and catchy choruses finds a delicate Davis howling in anguish at daring not to get too close to a lover for fear that they may stop loving him. Unsurprisingly chosen as a single, perhaps due to its radio-friendly nature (not that it earned Korn any significant exposure), 'Need To' provides a bit of calm to proceedings while still capturing abrasive heaviness in all its glory.

'Clown' (Korn)

The first track to really create an atmosphere within a song, Davis' pent-up angst explodes on the scathing 'Clown', which was written about a set-to during one of Korn's early live shows. While playing in San Diego, the band was heckled by a member of the audience who took a swing at Davis after previously shouting obscenities at the band and telling them to go back to Bakersfield. The issue was quickly dealt with when Korn's manager, Larry Weintraub, knocked the man out, allowing the show to continue.

Providing a little bit of early comedy, as he did on many an occasion, Ross Robinson kept the tapes rolling to capture moments of discussion – whether friendly or otherwise. Before 'Clown' starts up, the band can be heard arguing with Silveria, who wasn't sure whether the song was starting after four clicks or no clicks, to which Davis can be heard saying with some slight agitation in his voice, 'Just fucking do it, dammit!' Once things get underway, the distorted guitars create an eerie feel as Davis delivers another vocal performance born out of anger. 'Hit me clown, because I'm not from your town', he spits, having the last laugh on the night of the incident, as well as having the last laugh overall, as 'Clown' became one of the most popular songs on the album, as well as in Korn's whole back catalogue in the years to come.

Despite the heckling incident providing the song's central meaning, the paralleled lyrical similarities with bullying provided the main focus for the music video. Set in a high school, Korn spend much of the video performing in a changing room while Davis gets soaked through from sitting on the floor in the showers, as a handful of jocks poke fun at him from above a wall. Cheerleaders are also featured, signifying the second of the two core groups widely known to commit bullying in school, and their inclusions can provide an all too real bout of stomach-churning anxiety for many a sufferer of such acts in the past.

A further performance shot finds the band surrounded by a wall of unkempt toy dolls, and a life-size clown, similar in look to the evil Pennywise from Stephen King's *It* also makes regular appearances. Once again, directed by 'McG', the high school focus on Korn's third music video was perhaps the first to really reel in fans through the harsh and hospitable song lyrics that Jonathan Davis wrote for a generation begging to find their own forms of salvation.

'Divine' (Korn)

Containing thick and meaty verses, 'Divine' also has one of the catchier singalong choruses, but overall, it lacks the power and effect of those which came before and after it. Somewhat of a filler track, had Korn used the guidance given them by Suicidal Tendencies (and latterly Metallica) bassist Robert Trujillo, a little better, perhaps 'Divine' could have been what the title suggests. Still, most bands would kill to have a song like this within the track listing of their very best album, so it perhaps shows just how much quality Korn possessed from their humble beginnings.

'Faget' (Korn)

Written not long after Davis joined the band, Welch came up with the lead riff while sitting around in Korn's shared Huntington Beach house, and the rest, as they say, is history.

The most impressive song on the album and arguably just as important as 'Blind', 'Faget', really separated Korn from the rest of the pack with a rallying cry unleashed at bullies and tormentors. Revisiting his time in high school where he was teased and harassed for using eyeliner, listening to new wave music such as Duran Duran, and dressing a little more in-keeping with the New Romantic scene, Davis fights back at all those who accused him of being gay in an emotional tour-de-force which features some of Korn's most memorable vocal lines. Evil guitar rhythms and earth-shattering bouts of instrumentation make the song more of a colossus, as Welch and Shaffer show off what they called the 'Mr. Bungle chord'- playing two notes three steps away, in an ode to the experimental Mr. Bungle which was fronted by Faith No More's Mike Patton.

Acting as a voice for the voiceless, Davis fires through line after line of pent-up frustration, which includes 'I'm just a pretty boy, I'm not supposed to fuck a girl', and the fractious cries of 'I'm just a faggot!'. Robinson's raw production emphasises the true power 'Faget' possesses, helping create an everlasting legacy for a song that held more meaning than any other song on Korn, or at least until 'Daddy' came along.

While a music video was filmed for 'Faget', it never received an official release. The 'McG' directed short featured the full near six-minute song, and despite there being a lot of Adidas promotion once again, the video is a simple band performance in a bright room. Not as bold as the videos to come before it, it still showed Korn's progression and comfort at being in front of cameras, putting on an authentic presentation that best shows David Silveria's incredible drum prowess.

'Shoots and Ladders' (Korn)

Proving divisive between fans and critics – some calling it lazy, containing a lack of depth and being poorly executed, it is perhaps a testament to Korn that as young musicians still finding their way in 1994, 'Shoots and Ladders' would quickly become somewhat of a cult classic.

A heavy metal song that opens with some bagpipes was a first, and it was another instance of Ross Robinson's knack for catching the band off guard by keeping the tapes rolling. Picking up Davis walking past the studio door while playing the bagpipes as the mic remained stationary, what we hear gives the impression of Davis being farther away than he was before he does indeed move off into the distance. Interestingly, Davis first learned to play the bagpipes when he was in high school, where he has previously said he would play them for up to six hours a day. When Korn were hanging out during band practice one day, David Silveria told Davis to start playing the bagpipes in front of everyone, and only then did they decide to integrate them into a song, and 'Shoots and Ladders' made for their perfect debut.

Another revolutionary moment in metal and featuring lyrical renditions of children's nursery rhymes, Korn chose those with hidden and negative meanings behind them. 'All these little kids sing these nursery rhymes, and they don't know what they originally meant,' said Davis in a later interview. 'Everyone is so happy when singing 'Ring Around the Rosie', but it is about the Black Plague. All of them have these evil stories behind them.'

Also including parts of 'One, Two, Buckle My Shoe', 'London Bridge is Falling Down', 'This Old Man', 'Baa, Baa Black Sheep', and 'Mary Had a Little Lamb', 'Shoots and Ladders' is performed with a nightmarish sentiment which eradicates any small lingering moments of innocence. Leading to a final blast of violent instrumentation while Davis delivers more chaotic vocal refrains, 'Shoots and Ladders' earned the band their first Grammy Award nomination in 1997 for Best Metal Performance – despite its original mixed reaction. Pitted against prime cuts from Pantera, White Zombie, Rob Zombie and Alice Cooper, and the winning Rage Against the Machine, it was still an impressive feat when you consider Korn was already standing alongside such distinguished acts with many more years of experience under their collective belts.

Korn's second music video was again directed by 'McG' and partly using live show footage in which the band can be seen growing ever more comfortable on big stages they were playing during some vital support slots in their early days. In keeping with the song's meaning, though, it is the fairy-tale set containing a castle, waterfalls, trees, plants and colourful doll-like houses, which gives 'Shoots and Ladders' a visually spectacular music video. A radio edit sees the song reduced from 5:22 to 3:39 and thus removes much of the bagpipe intro, but the tension matched against the overly dream-like and innocent setting makes this very much a video not to be viewed by children. Another colourful and poignant moment in Korn's breakout, the band's music videos were already hinting at having a life of their own, where budgets were not going to be a problem in helping create a visual aspect to stand side by side with the power of their music and lyrics.

'Predictable' (Korn)

Another track considered by some as filler, the grunge influence of Alice in Chains shines through on this slow churning number performed in a lower key to the demo version on *Neidermayer's Mind*. While it is always good to change tempo and mix things up a little, 'Predictable' still showcases Korn's diversity, but the demo version does seem to have that something extra which this rendition is missing. With a safer vocal performance and an overall generic metal feel, this is one of, if not, *the* least effective songs amongst the twelve.

'Fake' (Korn)

Perhaps the song which gives an indication of where Korn might progress in the future with parts of their songwriting craft, 'Fake', features some of the best guitar work from Welch and Shaffer's potent combo, who clearly have a cohesive relationship after their years of playing together. A strong chorus finds Davis back on form after the less inspiring 'Predictable', and Silveria's drumming hits the spot with some strong time changes and cacophonous blasts. Full of funky heaviness, 'Fake' is one of the album's most underrated songs, and it still sounds impactful today.

'Lies' (Korn)

Containing a tasty opening riff before things settle down in the verses, things take a twisted turn when Welch takes over the vocal position with a southern twang on a punishing chorus, backed up by a death metal growl from Davis. Another gem of a song, which often gets forgotten due to the focus on 'Blind' and 'Faget' especially, 'Lies' finds Korn at their energetic and hostile best.

'Helmet in the Bush' (Korn)

Finding Korn messing around with electronics and drum machines to create an industrial-tinged stomp, 'Helmet in the Bush' is also the cleanest produced track, and it sounds absolutely huge. Another song written while under the influence of meth, the title of which alludes to penis shrinkage due to overdoing it with illegal drugs, 'Helmet in the Bush' finds Davis (and other members) begging God to help them kick their habit, as the line 'Please, God, don't let me give in tonight' suggests. Thick chugging riffs and some excellent rattling hi-hats make way for subtle melodies, making this a well-crafted number which once again showed Korn's willingness to try new things whether they were a success or not. In this instance, the result was overwhelmingly positive.

'Daddy' (Korn, Dennis Shinn)

And then came 'Daddy', the final song on Korn, and the most jaw-dropping piece of music released in all of 1994 and long after. Originally titled 'Follow Me', and written during Davis' days with SexArt, the initial concept once again coming from Dennis Shinn, Korn reproduced 'Follow Me', and Davis inserted his own horrific experience of being molested as a child by a family friend (and not his own father as the title suggests).

While the rest of the band had no prior knowledge of Davis's story ahead of recording, they would end up witnessing their singer cry and howl for a sustained period of time at the track's finale, shouting and berating his abuser and finally letting his pain out for the world to hear – spurred on by the relentless antics of Ross Robinson.

Set to more sinister guitar tones and a crunching bass line, the frankly shocking lyrical content takes precedence over anything else here, as line after line of unimaginable terror eventually leads to Davis' aforementioned breakdown.

While the Shinn-written version focused on an older person's perspective as they are about to do the abusing, Davis channelled his own desperate experience to give 'Daddy' a whole new meaning born out of reality. As he cries, a lullaby can be heard in the background being sung by Judith Kiener, which adds further atmosphere, while the band has their own little jam session, until a door is heard closing and all falls silent. Unsettling and emotional for everyone who hears it, 'Daddy' is the final stamp on one of the most original albums ever created, as it saluted Korn's arrival with the boldest of statements.

Life Is Peachy (1996)

Personnel:
Jonathan Davis: vocals, bagpipes
Brian 'Head' Welch: guitar
James 'Munky' Shaffer: guitar
Reginald 'Fieldy' Arvizu: bass guitar
David Silveria: drums
Record label: Immortal, Epic
Recorded at: Indigo Ranch Studios, Malibu, California, USA, April-July 1996
Produced by: Ross Robinson
Release date: 15 October 1996
Highest chart positions: US: 3, UK: 32
Running time: 48:14

> It really felt like we could do no wrong. Everyone was into what we were doing and really enjoying all the different styles we were putting into the music. It was a great time – a fucking crazy time, but a great time.
> Jonathan Davis

Korn's whirlwind adventure continued straight into album number two, which more often than not and especially in the unforgiving world of the music industry, is considered a band's make or break release. After such a pulsating start, Korn had to keep the momentum going whether they wanted to or not, and despite frequent fighting amongst themselves and heavy party sessions during recording and rehearsals, Korn fought their way out the other side with *Life Is Peachy*.

Featuring some natural progression from their first record, Korn returned with an album more abrasive and thrashier, although there were also more hooks and accessibility to the material on show. There were a lot of high points, but there were also some flaws; however *Life Is Peachy* was still urgent, scathing and unapologetically Korn.

Returning to Indigo Ranch with Ross Robinson in April 1996, the band didn't have much material to work with in the beginning, so instead, Welch, Shaffer, Arvizu or David Silveria would come up with an idea, whether it be an opening riff, a mid-song rhythm, a cool drumbeat, and the others would build on it from there. A collaborative process – most definitely, the usual way of creating music – not so much.

With *Korn*, Robinson elected for a warm and fuzzy analogue sound; however *Life Is Peachy* felt colder and harsher, but also more clinical. Taking elements of their first album as well as finding inspiration from their Indigo Ranch location and revisiting moments from the last two years of being on the road, Korn created cathartic music, which also featured a more prominent hip-hop influence, and on 15 October 1996, *Life Is Peachy* was released amongst a load of hype and expectation. Dealing with themes such as drugs (which were still a big issue for the band), social encounters, sex, and revenge, *Life Is Peachy* was an expectedly angry album and Jonathan Davis' vocal performances were just as primeval as those on the album previous.

Gaining mixed reviews, some suggested the album had been rushed while others focused on the filler tracks instead of the true highlights, but still, *Life Is Peachy* sold 106,000 copies in its first week in the US and went straight to number three on the *Billboard* 200.

Over the course of the album's cycle, 'No Place to Hide', 'A.D.I.D.A.S.' and 'Good God' were the three choices of singles – all of which fared better in the UK charts than in America by reaching 36, 22 and 25, respectively. 'A.D.I.D.A.S.' did hit 13 on the Bubbling Under Hot 100 Singles in America, though.

To help push *Life Is Peachy* out to the masses, Korn embarked on solo shows, headline shows with the support of Helmet and the up-and-coming Limp Bizkit, and the five-piece also supported Metallica on an arena tour which ran from late 1996 and into 1997. Venturing over to Australia and New Zealand was a first for the band (in May 1997), and then a return to Europe in the summer saw Korn hit various festival stages. After returning home, they joined the US stint of Lollapalooza; however, they would have to cancel much of the second half of dates after Shaffer was diagnosed with viral meningitis.

Continuing the innocent but threatened child theme, *Life Is Peachy's* cover art depicts a young boy smartly dressed and looking into a large mirror, seeing a much taller and stockier figure standing behind him. In some ways darker than the artwork for *Korn* due to the usage of black and white instead of colour, the photo was taken by Martin Riedl and its design and concept was created by Scott Leberacht. Interestingly, the album also includes Korn's logo in a different font, and it remains the only Korn album in their whole discography to feature this style, as the band would return to using their original and far more appealing logo for their next album and beyond.

Life Is Peachy has been certified double platinum in the US, and while the term 'Nu Metal' was yet to fully etch itself into heavy metal history, Korn had pretty much completed its blueprint with their sophomore album. Or so we thought.

'Twist' (Korn)

A rabid start in and out in less than 50 seconds, 'Twist' welcomes Jonathan Davis in full scat mode where the only audible word is the song title. Barking bile more incoherently than his short burst of drivel on 'Ball Tongue', in many ways, 'Twist' is the perfect album opener. Welch's shrieking guitar tones are there, Arvizu's slapping bass takes a prominent lead, and Silveria's groovy drum sections provide a taste of what is to come on another rough and ragged album very much in the same vein as the one which came before it.

'Chi' (Korn)

Its title in reference to Deftones bassist, Chi Cheng, with whom Korn were good friends at the time, as they were with the whole of the Sacramento quartet, 'Chi' shows hints of Korn's prosperous songwriting skills. Lyrically focusing on alcohol and drug abuse, Davis roars, 'Sick of the same old thing, so I dig a hole, buried pain' on a robust and fiery chorus.

The guitars are heavily distorted, and the clicky-sounding bass lines are still strange to hear, as 'Chi' shows Korn remain embroiled in dark and twisted metal. A song that would not have been out of place on the debut album, Ross Robinson's production stamp is all over it, while a nice switch from a heavy middle section to a soft and slow interlude finds the band taking a short breath before one final onslaught of energetic precision rounds things off nicely.

'Lost' (Korn)

Driving riffs and mature drum sequences sees 'Lost' elevate Korn to the next level with an excellently crafted alternative metal anthem. Clearly still full of pent-up angst, Davis demonstrates his flourishing vocal diversity, where he appears to have more control and focus in his voice at this time. Written about his sadness at being cast aside when a good friend of his meets a girl and chooses to spend all his time with her, it has been reported that the friend in question was actually Brian Welch, and during this time, Davis would only see him when the two were in the studio together. Largely unheralded because of the popular trio of singles, 'Lost' is a fine album track, up there with the best moments of the whole album.

'Swallow' (Korn)

A storming opening guitar assault gets the juices flowing straight away, featuring riffs imitated many times since by countless Korn wannabes. The hip-hop-tinged verses plod along with simple little guitar tweaks as Davis delves into lyrical themes based on drug-induced paranoia. A standout chorus full of brash but appealing instrumentation is the high point, before 'Swallow' fades out with Davis calling himself a 'punk ass sissy', which isn't really in keeping with the raw power that came before it. A great song, slightly let down by its underwhelming finale.

'Porno Creep' (Korn)

Super fuzzy guitars drowned in distortion and subtle pinches lead this jazz and funk interlude, but compared to what came before it, it does seem a little out of place. Inextricably Korn from just one listen, though, this two-minute track could easily have been cut in half to let the listener quickly move on to what comes next.

'Good God' (Korn)

Back on form from the off, 'Good God' is a stone-cold Korn classic. Written about a former friend of Davis who tried to make the frontman do things he didn't want to do, as well as sabotaging dates with potential love interests,

Davis puts his vocal cords on notice as he screams and rasps his former friend to 'get the fuck out of my face, now'.

Some deliciously haunting melodies give a great chorus further impact, taking 'Good God' from metal powerhouse to radio-friendly at the flick of a switch. Davis' later blast of the above lyric must have left him needing a Strepsil or two, such is the deafening anger he spits on the first true highlight of *Life Is Peachy*, which also showed the band were ready to embrace their incoming superstardom.

'Mr. Rogers' (Korn)

The most intriguing and creative song on the album, 'Mr. Rogers' was written about the former children's show host, Fred Rogers, whose program, *Mr. Rogers' Neighborhood*, was loved by parents and children across America from its very first episode, which aired in the late 1960s. Teaching his young viewers valuable life lessons about kindness and acceptance, Rogers becomes the target of Davis' maniacal ambush, which took him over three months to write – at the height of his drug troubles.

Realising the things Rogers taught were not true in the real world, Davis lays a small portion of blame at the TV star's door for the bullying he suffered in high school, which he was left unprepared for. His attack is delivered with abrupt and vicious screams of despair, as well as a small section of rapping, which was a first back then – further elevating the frontman's talent and notoriety.

A dark number featuring some ambient guitar rhythms and an unhinged but absorbing chorus, Davis lets his drug-induced psychosis get the better of him, which in truth helps make this song all the more spectacular. Whether Rogers himself ever heard the song before his death in 2003 remains unknown, and it is also interesting to know that Korn has never played 'Mr. Rogers' live. In 2000, the band asked their fans to vote for which songs should be included in their upcoming setlist, and despite this track being a popular request, Korn still refused to play it.

'K@#ø%!' (Korn)

One of those songs which Davis might look back on one day and say to himself, 'what was I thinking?', 'K@#ø%!' ('Kunts!' if you weren't sure) is a vile track possessing countless uses of vulgarisms aimed at women who had hurt the singer. Puerile lyrics where body parts are called by a plethora of different names, this is certainly a track that took away from the more creative and memorable numbers which were also found on *Life Is Peachy*.

Although the instrumentation is decent and led by more distorted and punchy riffs, it is hard for this 'song' to be considered anything other than the joke that it is. Apparently, Korn intended to send 'K@#ø%!' to radio stations in the US because of how they had edited previous songs, and you can only imagine how it would have sounded on the airwaves during the daytime, probably more like an instrumental with the number of bleeps they would have to have added. Not one of Korn's finest moments and ultimately one of their weakest tracks of all.

'No Place to Hide' (Korn)
The album's lead single and the song which would earn Korn their second Grammy Award nomination in 1998 (in the Best Metal Performance category, eventually won by Tool's 'Ænema'), 'No Place to Hide' features a generally softer approach. Its verses flow with just Davis' vocals and a simple drum beat and minute bass riffs, as the occasional guitar rhythm fights its way through, and although the chorus follows in similar fashion, it showed Korn's songwriting was progressing nicely on this imperative listen.

A heavier middle section sets pulses racing in true Korn fashion, and although it failed to chart in America, 'No Place to Hide' did reach 26 in the UK singles chart before getting the Grammy nomination some sixteen months after its original release. A formidable Korn song which has well and truly stood the test of time, its lyrical theme once again appears to focus on child abuse, as the disheartening line of 'You wanna touch me to see what's in my eyes' attested to Davis needing music to act as his own personal therapy even from very early on.

'Wicked' (O'Shea Jackson)
Showing off their love of hip-hop, Korn were joined by Deftones vocalist, Chino Moreno, to put their own spin on the Ice Cube song taken from his gold-selling album, *The Predator*, from 1992. Supplying plenty of funky and groove-orientated instrumentation, Moreno takes over lead vocals and he does a good job supplying the rap charge, while Davis scats and slays on an alternative chorus to the original version. Hip-hop beats and urban guitar textures illustrate how Korn were not scared to mimic one of their primary influences, on a version of 'Wicked' which the band, and Moreno, make their own to a certain degree.

'A.D.I.D.A.S.' (Korn)
Probably the most radio-friendly song on the album despite the song title standing for 'All Day I Dream About Sex', 'A.D.I.D.A.S.' was another future fan favourite from the beginning. Arvizu's bass guitar sounds enormous on this one, and its chorus was just begging for crowd participation in the live environment due to its singalong capabilities.

Including some of Welch and Shaffer's typical high-pitched guitar pickings and a drum section to die for, 'A.D.I.D.A.S.' is over and out in a little over two-and-a-half minutes, which was more than enough time to create its own personal legacy. The best performing single of the three released in the UK and America, it also boosted Adidas clothing sales all around the world despite the song having more to do with activities that didn't involve wearing any clothes whatsoever. It's funny how things turn out sometimes.

Out of the three singles released from *Life Is Peachy*, 'A.D.I.D.A.S.' was the only one to have a music video filmed, and it took Korn to the next level courtesy of Joseph Khan's treatment. 'When I finally got a rock video like Korn, it was fun to take my slick hip-hop sensibility and turn it loose on angry white guys', he said in a later interview. The video's plot revolves around a car crash in which a pimp and his prostitutes kill the five band members. Once the crash site is secured, Korn are placed into body bags, and during their transportation to the mortuary, and thanks to some highly effective make-up and CGI, the band members are seen violently wriggling around for added shock value.

In somewhat of a role reversal for ex-mortician Davis, he himself ends up on the table and when his customised sequined Adidas tracksuit is removed, he is found to be wearing women's underwear – further enhancing the sexual lust theme which 'A.D.I.D.A.S.' possessed.

A lot of money and detail went into a video that only lasts 150 seconds, and as much as it did for Korn, Khan's career also elevated from there as he would go on to direct videos for Rob Zombie, Papa Roach, Blink-182, Wu-Tang Clan, Eminem, Elton John and George Michael; to name just a few.

'Lowrider' (War, Jerry Goldstein)
A one-minute filler cover welcomes the bagpipes for a cameo appearance. Welch supplies the vocals on Korn's rendition of the popular War song, which originally starred on the funk band's 1975 album, *Why Can't We Be Friends?* More of an interlude than anything else and although initially thought to be oddly placed in the track listing, it does give the listener a sense that although *Life Is Peachy* is coming to a close, there is something explosive approaching just around the corner. 'Lowrider' is good for what it is, but generally, it is nothing more than another throwaway track.

'Ass Itch' (Korn)
Opening with a similar guitar flurry to 'A.D.I.D.A.S.', 'Ass Itch' documents Davis' issues with songwriting ('I hate writing shit, it is so stupid'), but it is another song based around an impressive hook-laden middle section. Frequent and nervy cries of 'pain' tell you what Davis' main lyrical influences revolve around, while Silveria's spirited drumming steals the show and further emphasises his talent. Showing that the best songs don't have to be fitted into the top half of an album's track list, 'Ass Itch' finds Korn with a second wind and plenty of craft left in them as *Life Is Peachy* goes deep into the fourth.

'Kill You' (Korn)
No Korn album closer will ever be remembered as much as 'Daddy', however, Davis has more anger and horror to unearth as this time, he takes aim at his former stepmother. In an interview years later, Davis was quoted as saying, 'She's the most evil, fucked up person I've met in my whole life...', and his tirade documents the things he would dream about doing to her – the

worrying chorus revealing his urges to beat, stab, fuck and kill his father's then-partner.

'Kill You' is another unsettling number that leaves the listener stunned, but perhaps that is what people were coming to expect from the band even in the early days. Forging some relentless instrumentation for one final bout of destruction, Silveria's drumming leans on the industrial side as Arvizu's bass tones take centre stage once again, while Welch and Shaffer combine nicely on one more furious guitar salvo.

Once 'Kill You' ends, a period of silence ensues before an acapella version of 'Twist' draws *Life Is Peachy* to an end. In the years which have passed, Korn's sophomore album has proved a divisive one amongst fans, but upon its release back in 1996, it was considered a good follow-up to the band's earth-shattering debut, although not quite as fulfilling.

Follow the Leader (1998)

Personnel:
Jonathan Davis: vocals, bagpipes
Brian 'Head' Welch: guitar
James 'Munky' Shaffer: guitar
Reginald 'Fieldy' Arvizu: bass guitar
David Silveria: drums
Record label: Immortal, Epic
Recorded at: NRG Recording Studios, North Hollywood, California, USA, March-May 1998
Produced by: Steve Thompson, Toby Wright
Release date: 18 August 1998
Highest chart positions: US: 1, UK: 5
Running time: 70:08

If *Korn* was the album to make a statement of intent and *Life Is Peachy* was the album to consolidate an upward trajectory, then *Follow the Leader* was the album that turned Korn into global megastars while at the same time launching Nu Metal headfirst into the mainstream.

Of course, Korn was already a pretty big deal come 1998, so much so that they also had many detractors – some of them being worried parents. Teenagers could regularly be seen wearing the latest t-shirts of their new favourite band, and one young man, in particular, suffered more than most because of his musical persuasion. 18-year-old Eric Van Hoven was suspended from his Zeeland, Michigan high school back in early 1998 for wearing a t-shirt that simply possessed Korn's logo on it, and it didn't go unnoticed by the school's assistant principal.

Making national headlines due to the teenager's unfair treatment, Gretchen Plewes made a statement to a local newspaper, *The Holland Sentinel*, in which she was quoted as saying Korn was 'indecent, vulgar, obscene, and intends to be insulting. It is no different than a person wearing a middle finger on their shirt.' MTV picked up the story and interviewed Van Hoven, and after his one-day suspension, he was soon removed from school again, for two days this time, after wearing a Tool t-shirt. Hearing about the story, Korn stepped in to further antagonise Plewes by donating t-shirts to the Greenville, Michigan radio station, WKLQ, who dished out the merchandise outside the school. The band also filed a cease-and-desist order against Plewes and threatened a multi-million-dollar lawsuit, but Korn would drop both actions because they had bigger fish to fry.

And that bigger fish was *Follow the Leader*, Korn's third studio album and one which had a cleaner and bigger production, plenty of groove and humble melodies, memorable choruses and dynamic rhythms. Moving away from Ross Robinson for the first time, Korn elected to work with Steve Thompson and Toby Wright; however, Robinson still had some input as he worked as Jonathan

Davis' vocal coach and continued to go to extreme lengths to get the best out of the singer.

Reportedly given over $750,000 to make the album, or maybe that is how much it cost by the end of it, party central continued as the band spent upward of $60,000 on booze alone. God knows how much went on drugs. In a 2013 interview, Davis reminisced on the recording session for the album's opening track, 'It's On!', 'People were getting blow jobs right behind me, there was girls banging each other in front of me, people getting boned in the closet behind me, it was the craziest shit I've ever seen in my life, and I sang that song.'

While Thompson produced three or four of the big songs on the album, Toby Wright took over and helped engineer and produce the record as Thompson was dealing with some personal issues at the time. Throwing himself in the deep end with a band who only appeared able to work while under the influence, Wright found out what he was up against when it came time to track vocals, which Davis only agreed to do if Wright met his demands of an eight-ball (a one-eighth ounce of cocaine, for the squeaky-clean folk out there).

One way or another, the album got recorded in North Hollywood, and, becoming one of the first bands to really utilise the internet in new ways, Korn documented the making of *Follow the Leader* through a weekly online show known as *KornTV*. Allowing fans to call in and ask questions, the show was successful in providing a close relationship between the band and their followers; and speaking of followers – the album's title.

With a band's success often comes envy, and imitators who want a piece of the action without putting in the hard graft, yet still they expect similar results. Korn witnessed these kinds of things happening in the wake of their rise to fame, and that is where the *Follow the Leader* title comes from, as the quintet intentionally upped the ante and threw a curveball at those who thought they could replicate Korn's formula. Many would try, but all would fail.

Ahead of the album's release, Epic threw a promotional party at Tower Records in New York City, and 9,000 people turned up for it. If Korn were still unsure of their popularity at this point, they had probably worked it out by the time the party wrapped up, as Davis recalled in a later interview with The Ringer, 'It was like being in The Beatles or some shit. That's when we were like, 'Ok, we're a big fucking band now'.'

Follow the Leader was released on 18 August 1998, and, to promote the album, the band launched a political campaign-style tour that took them all over the US via a chartered jet. Holding conferences, Q&A sessions and autograph signings, it all helped as Korn's third album sold close to 270,000 copies in its first week in America and went straight to number one on the *Billboard* 200. Korn's time was now.

As well as some promotional singles, 'Got the Life' and 'Freak on a Leash' were the two biggest cuts on the album, and both had big money music videos which received heavy rotation on TV channels in America and the UK especially. MTV's *Total Request Live* was the big show back in the late 1990s, and due to overwhelming demand for the two videos to be played over, and over again, 'Got the Life' became the first-ever video to be retired from the show; and 'Freak on a Leash' followed suit a few months later.

Containing another visually spectacular cover, however perhaps not quite so sinister as the art for both previous albums, renowned comic book artist Todd McFarlane was given the chance to create *Follow the Leader's* artwork. Along with other members of his team – Greg Capullo, Brian Haberlin and Brent Ashe – the comic book illustration shows a young girl hopscotching towards the edge of a cliff as a group of children are about to follow her. Part of the 'Freak on a Leash' music video would contain the cover's characters in an animated segment, intertwining with live-action shots and some dazzling special effects involving a travelling bullet. The video would win Korn their first Grammy Award for Best Music Video, as well as two MTV Music Awards for Best Rock Video and Best Editing. Everything was falling into place for the Bakersfield five.

To further promote the album, Korn embarked on their own Family Values tour, taking along Limp Bizkit, Ice Cube, Orgy, and Rammstein, while fellow up-and-comers, Incubus, replaced Ice Cube for the last four dates. Limp Bizkit's Fred Durst, and Ice Cube, both guested on songs on *Follow the Leader* (as did a few others), and they would join Korn on stage during the tour to perform the songs they featured on in front of jam-packed crowds every single night.

Follow the Leader remains Korn's most commercially successful album to date, its huge wall of sound and styles striking chords with metal fans both old and new. Going five times platinum in the US and amassing over fourteen million sales worldwide, Korn had fulfilled their potential and many people's expectations, with another classic metal album devoid of any traditional formula; and things would only get bigger and crazier from here.

'It's On!' (Korn)

A peer pressure anthem based around Jonathan Davis' excessive partying, which helped him forget his problems for a little while at least, as soon as 'It's On!' explodes into action, you can tell that the production of *Follow the Leader* sounds bigger and cleaner than Korn's previous efforts with Ross Robinson at the helm. Opening with a droning guitar effect and some hip-hop influenced percussion, further mighty guitar power and Arvizu's renowned bass kicks in to bring Korn's customary crunch, as swathes of electronic samples lurk in the background. Davis' cleaner vocals still contain a torturous underbelly, testing all areas of his voice box without ever sounding strained, while a stadium-sized chorus finds the band ready to go to the next level.

Original album pressings had 'It's On!' beginning at Track 13, as twelve tracks at five seconds in length each combined to have *Follow the Leader* open with a minute of silence for a fan of Korn who was losing his battle with cancer. A huge opening song which, like 'Blind' and Twist' on the albums before, found Korn making a huge statement from the off.

'Freak on a Leash' (Korn)

The song which saw the Bakersfield quintet go from young pretenders to global superstars – 'Freak on a Leash' built off the emphatic start of 'It's On!' by rewriting the formula of their first two albums, and re-routing and re-shaping their forward path as a band who stood a long way out from the rest of the crowd. Distorted and aggressive but still showing an air of accessibility, the most impressive chorus Korn had come up with to date finds Arvizu's still strange-to-hear bass-slapping breathe a new life of its own, while David Silveria also impresses with his ever-evolving drum skills.

Written about Davis' love/hate relationship with the music industry, where he felt he was being paraded around like a freak on a leash while label bosses and management were reaping all the benefits, his ferocious scat vocal drives the second half of the song into one final killer hook.

Sending heavy metal and the newly labelled Nu Metal movement headfirst into the mainstream eye, 'Freak on a Leash' reached ten on *Billboard*'s Mainstream Rock chart and 24 on the UK Singles chart – quickly earning silver certification with 200,000 units shifted. Having often been snapped wearing Adidas clothing since their inception, Korn signed a six-figure endorsement deal with the athletic brand Puma around this time. Puma were looking to break into Korn's youthful demographic, and although some fans saw this as Korn selling out, the band made no secret that they were cashing in. As part of the deal, 'Freak on a Leash' was used in TV commercials, and it was another funny side story to the rivalry between the two sports brands, as Adidas was founded by Adi Dassler, and Puma was founded by Adi's brother, Rudolf. By 2001, Korn had already moved on and signed a deal with Pony, which also had Limp Bizkit and Staind on its roster, and they even produced custom made kilts and shoes which Davis would wear when performing on stage.

Delivering their biggest video for what would be their biggest song, the music video for 'Freak on a Leash' proved to be a trendsetter for all future narrative-driven promos. Directed by Jonathan Dayton and Valerie Faris, and bookended by Todd McFarlane's incredible animation, which sees the characters from the *Follow the Leader* album cover come to life (kind of), the story begins with a policeman trying to stop a young girl from falling off the edge of the cliff during a game of hopscotch. When he falls and his gun accidentally fires, the bullet travels into the real world, where it blasts through a lava lamp, building walls, balloons, glass, water bottles; finally stopping in front of Jonathan Davis as Korn perform in a darkened room where the only light is from apparent bullet holes. Dancing and scatting in front of the bullet, it then returns to where it came from, the special effects and camera work providing innovative and powerful tension as it travels back into the original animated scene and the hopscotch girl catches it in her hand. With over 210 million views on the band's YouTube channel since its debut, this Grammy-winning music video isn't only considered Korn's best ever video but also one of the greatest music videos of all time.

'Got the Life' (Korn)

The obvious choice to be the album's lead single, 'Got the Life' raised a few eyebrows amongst Korn's hardcore following due to its overly commercial sound and its swaggering disco beats. Brian Welch:

It was so unique, and the more we sat with it and added to the song, we were like, 'Wow, this is crazy different. Let's go with this.' It ended up being one of the biggest hits. You've got to be open to trying new things in music is what that proved.

Also incorporating some rap elements as well as a triple-guitar overdub, the song's theme centres around the mixed blessings of fame, as its title hints at sarcasm rather than over-confidence. 'My mindset when I was writing the song was that I was really down on everything,' said Davis in later years. 'It's like I'm sick of this bullshit, all the stress and the pressure, but if it were all gone, I'd be in even more hell.'

Capable of getting people to sing along and dance to it in bedrooms and mosh pits all around the globe, 'Got the Life' reached 15 and 17 on *Billboard*'s Mainstream Rock Tracks and Modern Rock Tracks charts, respectively, as well as a healthy 23 on the UK Singles chart. It may not be as revered as 'Freak on a Leash', but 'Got the Life' is another classic within Korn's discography, its pop-tinged edge helping bring in new fans of both the band and heavy music in general.

Encapsulating Nu Metal's mainstream surge at the time, the music video for 'Got the Life' documented the money and fame that came with such lucrative record deals in the late 1990s. Returning to 'McG' for his directing skills, Korn also focused on the negative aspects of fame, as shown by Jonathan Davis' supposed breakdown in the back of a car while paparazzi surround him trying to get photographs. Attacking them with a baseball bat, while Arvizu gives away a swanky Mercedes to a valet and Shaffer and Silveria blow up a Ferrari, Korn were never more vocal in shunning such luxuries and those who were trying to follow in their footsteps. Instead, the video ends with a party with their closest friends and fellow musicians. Originally, the band approached Joseph Kahn with the video idea, having worked with him on the music video for 'A.D.I.D.A.S.', but he reportedly told them it was the 'stupidest idea I've ever heard'. Going back to 'McG', the future filmmaker thoroughly embraced the idea, which Arvizu had come up with. Highlighting how Korn may have been living the dream even though their new lives clearly weren't all they were cracked up to be, the music video for 'Got the Life' proved to be an overwhelming success.

'Dead Bodies Everywhere' (Korn)

Only Korn could begin a song with a chilling intro which sounds like one of those jewellery boxes you wind up, or a child's toy box even, its unsettling tone made possible by Welch plucking the higher notes of his guitar with the use of a harmoniser effect. From there, downbeat riffs take over as 'Dead Bodies Everywhere' turns the heaviness up to eleven. Its crunching vigour could have easily seen this one feature on *Life Is Peachy*, although the experimentation with electronics and a pulsating breakdown shows how far the boys from Bakersfield had come since their 1996 release.

Jonathan Davis' father, who was more commonly known as 'Ricky', was a touring musician when his son was young, and 'Dead Bodies Everywhere' finds Jonathan remembering back to his father telling him he wanted something better for his son. Also including small hints of his former job as a mortician, Davis passionately and almost apologetically roars, 'You want me to be something I can never ever be', as he follows in his father's footsteps down the music path. This is riveting stuff, and even though his advice was ignored, surely Ricky was proud of his son in the end.

'Children of the Korn' (Korn, O'Shea Jackson)

Going full-on rap metal on this intriguing collaborative effort, hip-hop icon Ice Cube guests, and lays down some solid rhymes over some spicy guitar-driven choruses. The hip-hop percussion is top-notch, the heavier moments are bruising, and with the title taken from Stephen King's best-selling novel where 'Korn' was spelt with a 'C', this decent crossover song points the finger at parents who believed Korn were corrupting their sweet and innocent offspring.

Bringing hip-hop and heavy metal fans together, these kinds of collaborations became more prominent during the height of Nu Metal, and a day after *Follow the Leader* dropped, Ice Cube released his *War & Peace, Volume 1: The War Disc* album, which featured a guest spot from Korn on the song 'Fuck Dying'.

'B.B.K.' (Korn)

Combining massive groove and an overall harsher guitar sound, industrial elements are intertwined with Korn's signature substance on this underrated gem. Its title based on Davis' preferred name for Jack Daniels and coke – 'Big Black Cock' – 'B.B.K' (presumably replacing the 'C' with a 'K' like the band's name) finds the frontman dealing with the pressure of creating album number three while he drinks himself into oblivion.

Musically fascinating, especially the shrieking guitar tones from Welch and Shaffer, more scatting is also included for good measure, and it is one of Davis' best performances of his unusual but highly effective style. Although released as a promo single, it was not a surprise that 'Got the Life' and 'Freak on a Leash' took all the plaudits; however, 'B.B.K.' still received rave reviews within the Korn community and from a whole host of music critics.

'Pretty' (Korn)

While most of *Follow the Leader* contains the lyrical content listeners come to expect from Jonathan Davis, the most horrific moment comes in the form of

'Pretty'. Telling the equally heart-breaking and infuriating story of witnessing an eleven-month-old baby girl ending up in his Kern County mortuary having been raped and killed by her own father, Davis delivers sombre verses over some eerie, mid-paced instrumentation. Harmonious backing vocals add further devilish atmosphere, a powerful chorus includes the angry line of 'What a disgrace'; and once again, Korn had turned pain and anguish into staggeringly thought-provoking art.

'All in the Family' (Korn, Fred Durst)

The first track released to give fans a small idea of what the album was to sound like, a demo version was sent to radio – and while fans liked what they heard, it certainly wasn't an apt representation of the strength in depth that *Follow the Leader* possessed; quite the opposite actually.

Featuring Limp Bizkit vocalist, Fred Durst, whose own band was about to hit the big time with their 1999 mega-seller, *Significant Other*, 'All in the Family' is a light-hearted affair which sees Durst and Davis trade insults with lines becoming more and more childish and explicit as the song progresses. While the seven-string guitars sound good and the hip-hop drumbeats flow nicely, this is by far the lowest moment on an otherwise incredible heavy metal album. Originally, Cypress Hill's B-Real was supposed to guest star instead of Durst, but his record label wouldn't allow it, and after hearing the finished product, he probably breathed a huge sigh of relief by avoiding this train wreck.

When Korn toured *Follow the Leader* on their Family Values run, Durst and the rest of Limp Bizkit joined them on stage to perform this track. Sending crowds into raptures as Silveria and John Otto went head-to-head on their respectable drum kits, Arvizu and Sam Rivers bass battled, and Wes Borland went up against the unassailable tag team of Welch and Shaffer. In the live environment, 'All in the Family' worked, but on record, it was certainly hit and miss.

'Justin' (Korn)

'Someone's gonna die and his last thing he wants to do is come hang out with us, I truly freaked out. It's like, why would you want to meet me, what makes me so special?' Unable to fathom why indeed, Davis put pen to paper and wrote one of his most creative songs in dedication to a terminally ill child suffering from intestinal cancer, whose last wish was to meet Korn.

If you thought the one-minute silence at the start of the album was a nice touch, the band go above and beyond in delivering a powerful and emotive song that is corrosive in its heaviness; however, it also packs huge groove. Featuring some excellent vocal distortion and hints of psychedelia, 'Justin' is an underrated masterpiece and one of Korn's best-ever songs.

Taking on emotional subject matter and turning it into a behemoth of creative genius, Justin was thankfully able to meet his heavy metal heroes with the help of the Make-A-Wish Foundation.

'Seed' (Korn)

Six minutes of well-paced raw power, 'Seed' is what Davis calls his son, Nathan, on this ode to his then-newborn. Talking about his son's innocence compared to the turmoil Davis suffered throughout his own younger years, Davis questions whether he really needs fame as he considers his newfound responsibilities in caring and providing for his child.

Including a fiery breakdown and some more vocal babble delivered in Davis' customary frenzied state, 'Seed' is a solid addition to the track list without ever being anything more than that. Interestingly, the song has never been performed live, as certain guitar effects used in the recording of it were lost by engineers upon the completion of *Follow the Leader*. We all make mistakes.

'Cameltosis' (Korn, Tre Vant Hardson)

Another guest spot sees Tre Hardson from West Coast hip-hoppers, The Pharcyde, supply most of the lyrics to 'Cameltosis', and vocal on a song which looks at scarred relationships – hence the naughty play-on-words title. Hardson's rap verses are the best part, while a slightly understrength Davis appears on a chorus where he confidently claims, 'I cannot ever love another c**t'. Silveria's monstrous drum sections stand out; however, 'Cameltosis' lags behind the far more likeable Ice Cube collaboration, which emphasises that sometimes less is more.

'My Gift to You' (Korn)

The bagpipes finally make an appearance as the final track on *Follow the Leader* takes shape. Industrial-tinged heaviness is the order of the day on 'My Gift to You'– a twisted love song Davis wrote for his then-fiancée, Renee Perez, who asked her lover to pen a song about her.

Dark and with plumes of electronic undercurrents, Davis talks of killing his woman to take her out of this world, relayed with one of his best vocal displays and sapping all remaining energy out of him by the end of the song. At just over seven minutes in length, 'My Gift to You' is the perfect choice of closer, where one final onslaught of throbbing instrumentation officially rounds off this mouth-watering epic.

'Earache My Eye' (Tommy Chong, Cheech Marin, Gaye Delorme)

A hidden track long into the extensive play out of 'My Gift to You', 'Earache My Eye' is a cover of the Cheech & Chong track from their 1974 album, *Cheech & Chong's Wedding Album*. Naturally heavier than the comedy duo's version, Korn reportedly recorded this song in only two takes, with Davis playing the drums, Silveria playing bass, and Arvizu providing some backing vocals while Cheech Marin himself took on lead vocal duties. Given a healthy and modernised overhaul, 'Earache My Eye' is not a bad choice of cover or hidden track, as Korn once again showed their intent of doing things differently and putting their own spin on whatever task they took to hand.

'I Can Remember' (Korn)

Included as a B-side on the 'Got the Life' single, 'I Can Remember' contains a similar sound and formula to Korn's creativeness circa 1998; however, the band deemed it unfit to feature on *Follow the Leader*. Laid back and low key, the song finds Jonathan Davis attempting to heal scars created by a broken friendship, as he once again alludes to the negative aspects of fame and success. Driven by simple percussive bass work which underpins Davis' double-tracked vocals, and also featuring the genre fusion which separated Korn from the rest of the crowd, 'I Can Remember' is a boisterous song that could easily have been included on the album had the quintet held it in higher regard.

Issues (1999)

Personnel:
Jonathan Davis: vocals, bagpipes
Brian 'Head' Welch: guitar
James 'Munky' Shaffer: guitar
Reginald 'Fieldy' Arvizu: bass guitar
David Silveria: drums, percussion
Record label: Immortal, Epic
Recorded at: A&M Studios, West Hollywood, California, Southern Tracks
Recording, Atlanta Georgia, USA, July-September 1999
Produced by: Brendan O'Brien
Release date: 16 November 1999
Highest chart positions: US: 1, UK: 37
Running time: 53:16

So, what do you do when you have released the biggest and most successful album of your careers so far – you go and tour the hell out of it for a couple of years. Not in Korn's case. Of course, there was the Family Values tour which went down extremely well, but by May 1999, the quintet was already getting to work on their next record, which, from very early on, had the title of *Issues*.

It is aptly named, because by now, Jonathan Davis had got himself sober. However, he was suffering bouts of crippling paranoia and nervous breakdowns, as well as going through a divorce from his partner of eight years, whilst becoming disorientated by his band's mainstream success. Sadly, the tales of overcoming the odds could not be said for the rest of the band, as Welch especially ventured further down the spiral with his heavy reliance on methamphetamine.

By the middle of July, Korn had already put most of the album together, so much so that during the legendary and controversial Woodstock festival of 1999, versions of new tracks 'Falling Away from Me' and 'Beg for Me' were aired at the show. Performing to an estimated crowd of an incredible 250,000, and second on the bill only to British rockers Bush, it is unsurprising that Davis still considers Woodstock to be his favourite show he has ever performed.

The first Korn album not to feature Ross Robinson in any way, Brendan O'Brien was taken on to produce *Issues*. Having worked with the likes of Pearl Jam, The Black Crowes and Rage Against the Machine, O'Brien was the kind of person who didn't suffer fools easily, his methodical and professional nature helping to create a more focused record due to not letting Korn party as much when they were in the studio.

Maintaining the band's core heaviness while also incorporating quirky guitar hooks, finer vocal melodies, experimental electronics and staccato riffing, *Issues* proved to be a divisive album amongst Korn's ever-growing fanbase. David Silveria called the album and its music 'simplified and heavier' in comparison to *Follow the Leader*, while reviews that came in ahead of its release used words such as 'melancholic', 'agitative', 'sorrowful' and 'introspective' to describe the album's overall feel.

Issues featured five interlude tracks, created by Davis from the 'weird thoughts in my head', he told *Kerrang!* in 2002, and for the first time, there was no hidden track at the end. There were also no guest spots. 'Falling Away from Me', 'Make Me Bad' and 'Somebody Someone' were the three singles released, the first of which was the most successful. Debuting on an episode of the adult cartoon, *South Park*, in which the band are also featured performing the song, it would be almost two months before a physical release would be made available. Against the wishes of their management and record label, and furthermore proving how far the internet had come as the new millennium approached, Korn uploaded 'Falling Away from Me' onto their website as a free MP3, telling their fans to email the song to their friends and create a kind of chain mail. Fans were also encouraged to sign a virtual guestbook, as with each signature, the band would make a donation to two children's organisations. In the end, Korn raised over $250,000, and regardless of the freebie, the single still reached number 7 on *Billboard*'s Mainstream Rock Songs chart, and 24 in the UK Singles chart.

Another first saw Korn launch an MTV contest where fans had the opportunity to create the album's cover art. Receiving over 30,000 entries, the ragdoll image Korn fans have come to know was drawn by Alfredo Carlos, who won the $20,000 top prize. A further four designs were also used on various releases of the album, such as a special tour edition, while one was also used for the 'Make Me Bad' single release.

Released on 16 November 1999, *Issues* went straight to number 1 on the *Billboard* 200, with first-week sales of a whopping 575,000. Beating new releases from Dr. Dre and Celine Dion, it showed how much mainstream focus Nu Metal was getting, and within four weeks, *Issues* had already been certified triple platinum in their homeland.

On the eve of its release, Korn performed the album in its entirety at New York's Apollo Theater, and with it, they became the first white rock act to perform there since Buddy Holly in the late 1950s, as the venue traditionally hosted African American performers over recent times. Featuring a choir and the pipes and drums section of the New York Police Department, the show was broadcast live across radio stations and via a special webcast, with an estimated one million people logging on to witness Korn make history once again.

From February to August in 2000, Korn's Sick and Twisted Tour became one of the band's most successful tours of all time, travelling the world and playing some of the biggest venues of their career. Support acts included fellow Nu Metal bands such as Staind, Papa Roach and Powerman 5000, as well as Spike and Mike's Sick and Twisted Festival of Animation, which was an adult orientated animation made famous by being included in early episodes of Beavis and Butthead and South Park.

Issues has gone on to sell over thirteen million copies worldwide, second only to *Follow the Leader* – but not by much.

'Dead' (Korn)

A subdued intro kicks off the album with Jonathan Davis' bagpipes making an early appearance over some marching band-style drumming. Davis doesn't sound any happier, leading a whispered chant of 'All I want in life is to be happy', while some orchestral sounding backing vocals already show Korn taking a different direction from what fans were used to hearing from them.

'Falling Away from Me' (Korn)

In true fashion, the first proper song on a Korn album becomes an instant classic, bulldozing its way into the listener's psyche as powerful riffing fires up the lead single. Arvizu's fuzzy bass lines sound emphatic, Welch's renowned high-pitched riffs create an eerie sense of unease in the verses, and David Silveria's groove-fuelled drum sections find his performances enhancing things further.

Based around domestic abuse and how there is always a way to get out of such a situation, 'Falling Away from Me' packs a punch with a chorus as big as the arenas Korn were now selling out, and Davis' vocals diversify between his delicate harmonies and the beefier blasts which are laden with passion and commitment. One of Korn's best songs and forever a staple in their live set, the track reached seven on *Billboard*'s Mainstream Rock chart and 24 on the UK Singles chart.

The accompanying music video topped MTV's *Total Request Live* on ten various days. Directed by Limp Bizkit's Fred Durst, Davis reportedly hated the frontman's treatment for it at first, but he was outvoted by his bandmates, and so Durst got the job. Picking up where the 'Freak on a Leash' video left off, live-action is restored and tells the story of a girl hiding from her abusive father in her bedroom. Watching Korn perform 'Falling Away from Me' inside a small music box, the band later explode out of it and into her bedroom, while neighbourhood children gather outside the house and encourage her to jump out of her window to escape her father, who frantically tries to kick down her door with a belt in hand. By the time he gets the door open, both the girl and Korn are nowhere to be seen, providing somewhat of a happy ending, which Korn didn't do too often.

'Trash' (Korn)

Possibly the best Korn song never to be released as a single but still good enough to make it onto their *Greatest Hits Vol. 1* compilation a few years later, 'Trash' finds Davis dealing with the opposite sex – loving and wanting the physicality, but without the emotional ties that come with it. It is in the instrumentation where 'Trash' really stands out, as melodies intertwine while Davis whispers away, before distorted and heavy guitar crunches elevate an enormous chorus to new levels. One of the better songs to show Brendan O'Brien's production talents and wanting the band to experiment a little more, he puts his stamp on a song that Korn would have never been able to come up with a year prior, and with a droning guitar effect which filters in and out of the whole song, 'Trash' is a dark, anthemic and absolutely monstrous number.

'4U' (Korn)

The droning guitar effect continues into this second interlude, which is a ballad of sorts where Davis shows his appreciation for his band's fans. A simple percussive beat, atmospheric guitar rhythms and bell chimes drive this two-minute interval along, as Korn stop thinking about their own issues for a little while and count themselves lucky for the position they find themselves in. If *Issues* found Korn at their most uncertain, '4U' found them at their most humane, as emphasised by the final line of 'I could have never lived, if it wasn't for you'.

'Beg for Me' (Korn)

Another self-expose from Davis, who admits to needing his fans and an audience in order to relieve himself of his anxiety for a short time, 'Beg for Me' is led by a vicious riff and more marching drum-esque deliveries. Shaffer's guitar effects zigzag in the background, and a rousing chorus thunders along even if it isn't quite as hooky as the previous two which came before it. Arvizu pushes himself further with some intriguing and challenging bass lines, on a song that is both combative and highly accomplished.

'Make Me Bad' (Korn)

Sometimes you can tell from the first few seconds which songs are ideal for single releases and which songs aren't, so it probably wasn't much of a surprise when 'Make Me Bad' was chosen as the album's second promo release. A tentative drum machine beat and more high note riffs welcome in a familiar Korn rampage before the verses become muted and disconcerting. Davis hints at his sorrow of the breakdown of his marriage, supplying sexual connotations such as adultery on another fruitful chorus where Arvizu's bass work shines brightest. Annoyingly catchy for something so downbeat and torturous, 'Make Me Bad' continues Korn's evolution in gripping fashion.

An *Alien*-inspired music video was filmed to accompany the single release, and it remains one Korn's most expensive videos ever made, due to the special effects used, as well as having popular Hollywood actors such as Udo Kier (Ace Ventura: Pet Detective, Barb Wire), Brigitte Nielsen (Red Sonja, Rocky IV), Shannyn Sossamon (A Knight's Tale, The Rules of Attraction), and supermodel Tatjana Patitz star in the short film.

Directed by Martin Weisz, the five band members are used as test subjects and locked in separate rooms before a kind of shock therapy is later used, and an ominous creature is seen lurking underneath their skin. Later revealed, when Davis has his stomach cut open and a doctor removes a small alien-like creature, this mini-movie of sorts ends on a cliff-hanger. While the 'Dead' intro can be heard, Kier and Nielsen appear to be plotting some kind of alien invasion, holding a similar creature in their hands, and presumably the ones who infected the band in the first place. A bit of a head-scratcher, but grandiose in its cinematic values, it was a sign of Korn's ever-growing popularity that such budgets were available to them to create increasingly vivid music videos. As with 'Got the Life', 'Freak on a Leash' and 'Falling Away from Me', 'Make Me Bad' became the fourth Korn video to become officially retired by *Total Request Live*.

'It's Gonna Go Away' (Korn)

Another interlude which this time airs on the side of the gothic, 'It's Gonna Go Away', has a short burst of dreamy guitar tones as Davis' howls and wails see him come off as melodramatic. The Cure meets Nine Inch Nails is pretty close to what you get on this short stab.

'Wake Up' (Korn)

Picking up the pace straight out of the gate, 'Wake Up' gets things back on track with some scarring instrumentation as heavy as anything else contained on the whole album. Along with Davis shouting 'Wake the fuck up', this song acts as one of the best alarms you could ever have beside your bed, such is the ferocity of the opening passage. Settling down for some dub groove verses a million miles from the robust intro and chorus, this is a clash of styles which, had Korn not come up with it, would probably never have worked.

Lyrically, Davis calls on his brothers in arms to leave their tension and egos at the door so they can continue to take over the metal world. With lines such as 'You are my brothers, each one I would die for', and the poignant 'Let's take the stage and remember what we play for', 'Wake Up' is an excellent number, which is no doubt relevant and relatable to many bands out there who have been in a similar position at some point or another in their careers. Great stuff.

'Am I Going Crazy' (Korn)

The least effective of the interludes, random samples lead a disorientating and almost psychedelic 60 seconds of filler, although you probably get an idea of what was going on inside Jonathan Davis' head during his bouts of paranoia, as it likely sounded a little something like this.

'Hey Daddy' (Korn)

Not a sequel to the disturbing finale of Korn, nor does it revisit the same subject matter, Davis refers to himself as 'daddy' as he describes the thoughts inside his head during the process of getting sober. Extremely funky and deceptive in its upbeat nature, 'Hey Daddy' may be tormented, but it offers moments of positivity as Davis fights his fears by simply living. The guitars are turned up to ten on a chorus delivered with precision, all the while driven along by Silveria's irresistibly mighty sounding drums. An unheralded success without doubt.

'Somebody Someone' (Korn)

Issues' most vicious track and packing industrial-tinged heaviness and distortion, 'Somebody Someone' also features some unique structures along the way. Davis provides his most aggressive vocals, again asking for support as his delicate mental state leaves him feeling worthless. A brutal breakdown takes centre stage midway through, while a great echo effect creates further potency on some of the vocals. The final single released from the album, 'Somebody Someone' may not have done much in the charts, but it was popular enough amongst Korn fans for it to regularly feature in the band's live sets for well over a decade.

While the accompanying music video was still a splendid watch, 'Somebody Someone' was given a slightly simpler but nonetheless effective treatment courtesy of Martin Weisz. Performance-based and filled with CGI, Korn perform the song in an underground bunker setting where spiders, cockroaches and flies join the band for company. Various shots from the view of a pesky fly are well crafted, and the moments of Davis' roars startling the bugs are also impressive, but due to the last four or five videos to come before it, this one was never going to raise the bar further.

'No Way' (Korn)

Plenty of experimental undertone's drive 'No Way' on a slow and sauntering song which still remains on the side of heavy, even though a predictable formula never really ignites into anything more. The shrieking riffs are still there, Arvizu's distinct bass lines dip in and out, but in general, 'No Way' is a typical later-in-the-track list kind of song which fills some space and fails to live up to the many high points which surround it.

'Let's Get This Party Started' (Korn)

The final sentence summing up 'No Way' certainly cannot be said here, as 'Let's Get This Party Started' is perfect for mosh pits and alternative dancefloors alike. Light and mildly funk-orientated verses sound even better with the creative vocal effects placed over Davis' deliveries, and a colossal chorus ups the ante with a rawness not as frequently visited on *Issues*. Davis talks of various ways to deal with his bouts of depression, but some of the song's meaning can easily get lost with the simplicity and addictive nature of a chorus which leaves you singing along on the first repeat.

'Wish You Could Be Me' (Korn)

The final interlude finds Davis recycling already documented fears of going insane over a simple drum beat and some skewed samples. A hyperactive throwaway.

'Counting' (Korn)

Taking the aggressiveness of *Life Is Peachy* and the groove of *Follow the Leader* to create a solid metal stomp worthy of its place on the album, 'Counting' also contains a jazz-tinged bridge that switches things up a little. The lines of 'Take advantage of what I feel' and 'One day you'll beg for me' indicate an attack on the music industry, while the terrific line of 'They give you money and the girls and the fame, I only do it for the fun and the games' cause goosebumps to rise on your arms as Davis lays it all on the line. Pressing forward in ending the album with a couple of bruisers, 'Counting' is the ideal beginning of Korn's second wind.

'Dirty' (Korn)

True to form, Korn round off another album with another spectacular finale. Slow-building verses create tension with the sense that something big is coming, and when a huge chorus drenched in distortion arrives with downbeat riffs, its earth-shattering nature finds Korn at their absolute best. 'I wish you could see the world through my eyes' Davis cries, ridding himself of any remaining energy and emotion by shouting and screaming as if his life depended on it. Industrial samples and intricate guitar rhythms add further layers, and with one final heroic hook, Issues ends on the grandest of notes with another enthralling anthem.

For the first time, there is no hidden track, as upon the conclusion of 'Dirty', four minutes of static is all that can be heard. It has been mentioned that Davis saw *Issues* as somewhat of a concept album, so we could take the static to symbolise the story's end, leaving us to think about what we have just heard and witnessed with contemplation and exploration.

Untouchables (2002)

Personnel:
Jonathan Davis: vocals
Brian 'Head' Welch: guitar
James 'Munky' Shaffer: guitar
Reginald 'Fieldy' Arvizu: bass guitar
David Silveria: drums
Record label: Immortal, Epic
Recorded at: Conway Studio, Hollywood, California, The Village, Los Angeles,
California, USA, April-November 2001
Produced by: Michael Beinhorn
Release date: 11 June 2002
Highest chart positions: US: 2, UK: 4
Running time: 65:00

Despite the overwhelming commercial success of *Issues*, some of the mixed reviews and fan reaction to it created some doubt as to whether Korn had already passed their peak, and so what better way to prove their doubters wrong than to come back with all guns blazing on their next opus. The longest period between any of the band's albums to this point, 31 months separated the release of *Issues* and *Untouchables*, where heightened expectation reached unparalleled levels when in early 2002, Korn announced a June release for their boldest and bravest effort yet.

With the Red Hot Chili Peppers, Soundgarden and Ozzy Osbourne amongst his credits, Michael Beinhorn was chosen to produce *Untouchables*; in fact, the album's writing process actually began almost a year before the release would see the light of day. Despite hostility and tension increasing between the band members, Beinhorn did his best to keep the ship steady. 'They are extremely talented,' he said of Korn in a 2019 interview with the BREWtally Speaking podcast, 'but they also have the most incredible case of collective ADHD I've ever seen. So it wasn't easy keeping them focused.'

Said to have cost around $4 million, with a large chunk of that money spent on the rental of houses for each of the five members for months at a time, as well as keeping their crew on retainer throughout the almost two years it took to complete the album, *Untouchables* was released on 11 June 2002. The day before, Korn performed a special album launch show at the Hammerstein Ballroom in New York, which was broadcast online and in movie theatres across America. Latterly, it was released as an official DVD.

Rich with swathes of savage riffing, nosebleed bass lines, punchbag drumming, as well as peculiar chords and strange harmonies, it was also the first Korn album not to feature any usage of the bagpipes. *Untouchables'* inception into the world was met with critical acclaim, selling close to 435,000 copies in its first week in the US alone. Had it been released at any other time than the first half of June, then it would have cruised straight to number 1 on the *Billboard* 200; however, hip-hop sensation, Eminem, had just dropped his latest album, *The Eminem Show*, and its second-week sales were enough to keep *Untouchables* off the top spot. In the UK, Korn scored their highest ever position of 4 in the country's album chart. Although it went platinum within a month of release, *Untouchables* slumped after its impressive first week, with many including Jonathan Davis blaming internet piracy. The album had leaked online more than two months ahead of its official release, and with illegal downloading crippling the music industry at the time, it appeared to signal the end of the way people knew the music industry to be.

Three singles were put out from the album – 'Here to Stay', 'Thoughtless' and 'Alone I Break', the first of which was sent to radio some four months ahead of the album's June release. In an attempt to re-ignite album sales, *Untouchables* was re-released five months later with different artwork and a bonus DVD, but it didn't really succeed in its intention other than giving hardcore fans the opportunity to add another Korn CD to their collections. From February through to August, Korn relentlessly toured to promote their latest release. Their first US run was subtitled The Tour With No Name, and the second fell under the Pop Sux Tour moniker, while a European stint took place in-between. Nu Metal bands such as Disturbed, Static-X, Puddle of Mudd, Deadsy and Trust Company were given support slots, and with it the chance to play in front of some of the biggest crowds of their careers.

Despite its disappointing sales, Davis has stated on many occasions that *Untouchables* is the album he is most proud of, and in a 2002 interview with *Noisey*, he alluded to its lengthy recording process where the vocals alone took almost six months to lay down: 'Beinhorn's whole vision was to make an amazing-sounding rock record that could never be made again. It was the peak and pinnacle of everything in Korn. I still can't believe how much work went into it.'

The album's cover was created by Eric White, his drawing showing various kids standing in a group, some with cuts and bruises on their faces. Somewhat symbolising Korn's legions of fans, it also incorporated the album's title meaning, which was in reference to the Caste System in India. A practice of ostracising a minority group by segregating them from the mainstream by either social custom or legal mandate, *Untouchables* was an instantly relatable album title that continued to find Korn and their fans taking on the rest of the world.

'Here to Stay' (Korn)

When you have spent so much time and money on an album, the pressure is on to show any potential detractors that the wait has been well and truly worth it; and Korn justified the meticulous preparation of *Untouchables* with the launch of 'Here to Stay'. A rampant and perfect choice of lead single, the quintet proved they hadn't lost their touch for writing powerhouse anthems worthy of the reputation which preceded them, opening with explosive downtuned riffing, a cataclysmic bass crunch and drum sections capable of causing earthquakes.

Any trepidation is quickly dispelled as the opening procession of instrumentation stands tall before Jonathan Davis steps in with his customary pain-induced vocal displays. Following a similar structure to 'Falling Away from Me', 'Here to Stay' contains one of Korn's greatest choruses, while a breakdown section slowly builds up to a punishing rock out complemented by the first aggressive roars from the frontman. Lyrically focusing on fighting back after being taken advantage of, 'Here to Stay' confirmed the Bakersfield five were exactly that, with a song so good that it won a Grammy Award in 2003 in the Best Metal Performance category. Reaching 12 in the UK Singles chart was also impressive, as was a 72 placing on *Billboard*'s Hot 100. Perhaps not as ground-breaking as 'Blind' or 'Freak on a Leash', but 'Here to Stay' rightfully deserves to be mentioned amongst Korn's greatest ever songs.

Backing up Korn's huge budget, a colossal music video for the lead single was an absolute must, and thankfully, The Hughes Brothers delivered for 'Here to Stay'. Going all out on an uncensored version which contained clips of violence, war, sex, gruesome surgeries, childbirth, animal attacks, nuclear explosions and police chases – to show just how much the outside world can distort a young person's mind with such negativity – it certainly wasn't a video for the faint-hearted. Drenched in static, Korn perform 'Here to Stay' on a TV set watched by a young boy in a garden shed, as he gets sucked into the set after he reaches out his hand to an inviting Davis. An edited video only shows the band's performance, but at least you have a choice of two if you are a little squeamish. A huge video to match a huge song.

'Make Believe' (Korn)

Taking a surprising turn so early, 'Make Believe' finds Korn trying something new to keep themselves well ahead of the curve. Boasting strange waves of glittering synth and multi-tracked twilight zone-like vocals, it was the most experimental and expansive the band had sounded to date.

Utilising the increasingly prosperous digital age to their advantage, perhaps thanks in part to having Michael Beinhorn at the helm, 'Make Believe' gathers momentum on a purposeful chorus where Davis appears to feel the need to justify his song lyrics against those who question whether his horrific past is make believe for personal gain. A strange song back in 2002 and still a strange song today, many fans struggled to get their heads around 'Make Believe' and so it perhaps remains one of the band's most underappreciated songs.

'Blame' (Korn)

Normal service is resumed on this absolute banger, focused around a gigantic riff and Arvizu's rattling bass work. Eerie synth pulls the verses along nicely while Davis' vocals are given a gothic effect, before the lead riff fires back up to perfectly accompany David Silveria's vaulting drum sections. The pre-chorus is stellar, the main chorus is classic Korn, and further bouts of obliterating instrumentation wraps up one of the highlights of *Untouchables,* which was most definitely single-worthy, had a fourth promo release been on the cards.

'Hollow Life' (Korn)

It is back to the weird and wonderful on the track which gives the first real indication of the huge amounts of money which went into making the album. Largely keyboard-based and overdosing on electronics, 'Hollow Life' is a dreamy sci-fi-like epic which finds Korn breaking the mould again. Davis' melodic vocals dominate this contemplative number looking at people's belief in God and not receiving help and guidance when they need it most.

A catchy hook and buoyant drums which are the most prevalent of the three key instruments, 'Hollow Life' is another ambitious song which the band felt they had to attempt in order to shake things up a little, having called the nu metal movement in 2002 'soulless'. Intriguing and successfully pulled off, no one saw this song coming from Korn back in the day.

'Bottled Up Inside' (Korn)

With the early track list shifting back and forth between heavy and experimental songs, it was unsurprising that 'Bottled Up Inside' returned to the angry and aggressive end of the scale. A straight-forward alternative metal romp where Davis' line of 'You raped and stole my pride, and all this hate is bottled up inside' showed the pain he possesses will never truly go away, this is a decent album track where its revenge theme could be aimed at both bullies and abusers alike.

'Thoughtless' (Korn)

Originally titled 'Tear Me Down', the words featuring in the song's gigantic chorus, 'Thoughtless' is another now-legendary Korn anthem and the second single to be released off *Untouchables.* Powerful and melodic, especially on its made-for-radio chorus, the song is driven by a staccato percussive riff and looks at the damage caused by people who are constantly ridiculed. Interestingly, Songfacts.com discusses the lyrics relating to the Columbine killers, Eric Harris and Dylan Klebold, who murdered twelve students and a teacher at their Columbine High School on 20 April 1999. Presented from their point of view and how they would get their own back on the jocks who had picked on them, the song's lyrics would become instantly applicable to many a kid who experienced bullying in their own lives; and of course, Davis himself suffered similar attacks during his own high school years.

The official music video, again directed by The Hughes Brothers, features a pre-*Breaking Bad* Aaron Paul as the protagonist, who gets his revenge on his bullies at the high school prom by vomiting his pent-up anger and frustration all over his aggressors. There have been reports of an alternative version of the video being filmed with the use of guns, but it remains unclear if it ever made it past the treatment stage. In the song there is a little bit of Davis' babbling, the double-stacked chorus is emphatic, and with an effective use of backing vocals, 'Thoughtless' quickly cemented itself as an instant fan favourite.

'Hating' (Korn)

Five minutes of dark and atmospheric rock containing squishy keyboards and offbeat guitar rhythms, 'Hating' pits various styles on another song which showcases Korn's songwriting progression. 'We are the stars' and 'I'll take what's mine' says Davis at various intervals, without ever sounding arrogant in the process. Another new direction ventured here, Korn took the task to hand with effortless ease and the results were there for all to see.

'One More Time' (Korn)

Recalling the disco vibes of 'Got the Life', 'One More Time' is an upbeat singalong that finds Korn rarely having to step out of second gear. 'It's basically about these feelings always chasing me, like I have an alter ego', explained Davis in a 2002 interview, and while the subject matter may sound quite dark, the music is a good counteraction in making this much more of a dancefloor filler than a mosh pit menace. Standard Korn, but a standard much higher than what most bands were coming out with back in 2002.

'Alone I Break' (Korn)

The first proper Korn ballad and penned by Davis after seeing his bandmates struggling with various personal issues, 'Alone I Break' is a beautifully crafted song with a hip-hop beat and subtle guitar riffs leading the verses, samples filling the space underneath; all delicately entwined before a tearjerker of a chorus demands your lighters to be raised.

The third and final single, its music video was filmed like a reality TV show which sees Davis killing off his brothers in arms one by one – electrocuting Shaffer while he is taking a bath, throwing Welch from a balcony, suffocating Silveria in a bed he is sharing with two lovely ladies, and poisoning Arvizu by putting something sinister in his food. MTV promoted a contest and program titled *mtvTREATMENT* where 25-year-old winner, Sean Dack, was chosen to direct the video. After a panel of judges from Epic Records chose the 21 best concepts, the finalists had to submit a video tape of themselves from which Korn chose the winner, and the resulting music video made for interesting viewing even if it took away the sensitivity of the song's true meaning.

'Embrace' (Korn)

Returning to their old school sound on this one, Welch and Davis provide dual vocals on a vicious number which is led by a chunky riff. By far the heaviest song on *Untouchables*, 'Embrace' has an *Issues* vibe on a chorus where tiny melodies drip from the hostility, while Davis also supplies some of his mightiest roars since his *Life Is Peachy* days.

'Beat It Upright' (Korn)

If you thought the band had completely grown up, then think again, as what could almost be considered a companion piece to 'A.D.I.D.A.S.' brings back the dirt both musically and lyrically. A grinding riff accompanies sadomasochistic lyrics, which includes the laughable lines 'ass up high, make a motherfucker cry' and 'Are you ready for a good pounding baby?'. It was hardly a surprise that the clean version of *Untouchables* neglected to include 'Beat It Upright' on its track list. The only song of the original thirteen to be omitted, and due to its less mature and underwhelming flow, possibly the one that was missed the least.

'Wake Up Hate' (Korn)

Seeped in gothic and industrial nuances, 'Wake Up Hate' is an urgent and rampaging song that finds Korn imitating others. Davis sounds a lot like Marilyn Manson with the spooky vocal tones on show, while gang vocals shouting *en masse* 'We're gonna fuck you up' cannot be taken seriously as the tough-guy persona doesn't suit them. Sharp and abrasive, its addition is still welcome no matter how safe and simplified the song comes across.

'I'm Hiding' (Korn)

Some interesting structures mix sauntering and spacy verses with a beefy chorus. Rough and low-end riffs make a triumphant return, and a nice vocal effect makes Davis' echoed refrains sound like he is singing in a fishbowl, but it is David Silveria who is the star of 'I'm Hiding', as he provides some thrash-tinged drumming which sounds almighty due to the crucial production work of Michael Beinhorn. No expense spared.

'No One There' (Korn)

Unlike the previous album closers, 'No One There' sees *Untouchables* bow out with a slow-burning metaller which lacks that 'going out with a bang' feel compared to 'Daddy' or 'Dirty', for example.

The kind of song you would hear while the end credits of a movie or TV show are rolling, Davis takes stock of his life once again and hints at an optimistic future with the line, 'I know it's time to leave these places far behind'. Heavy in places but generally more refined, 'No One There' might be a little less rewarding, but it is a decent way to end an album that, overall, can be considered a success. Whether it was worth $4 million is another story for another day.

After just six seconds of silence at the song's end, a remix of 'Here to Stay' brings back the hidden track feature. T-Ray's Mix, or anyone else's mix for that matter, was never going to be able to compete with the slamming original, and as this writer doesn't see the point in remixes in the first place, anyone hoping to hear an original Korn song or even a cover, were left with something of a bad taste in their mouth.

Take a Look in the Mirror (2003)

Personnel:
Jonathan Davis: vocals, bagpipes
Brian 'Head' Welch: guitar
James 'Munky' Shaffer: guitar
Reginald 'Fieldy' Arvizu: bass guitar
David Silveria: drums
Record label: Epic, Immortal
Recorded at: Elementree Studios, Tarzana, California, USA, April-June, August 2003
Produced by: Korn, Frank Filipetti
Release date: 21 November 2003
Highest chart positions: US: 9, UK: 53
Running time: 56:43

The fallout from *Untouchables'* disappointing sales and the bill Korn ran up during its recording process continued into 2003, resulting in the band going back into the studio and getting to work on their sixth album.

A back to basics record where Korn returned to their aggressive sound by utilising thick and heavily distorted guitars, *Take a Look in the Mirror* found the quintet struggling with their creativity. Forcing themselves to get to work while dealing with time restraints caused by being on the road and co-headlining Ozzfest 2003, the album was partly written on the band member's buses after playing live on many an evening. Produced by themselves in Jonathan Davis' home studio, Korn also sought the assistance of Michael Beinhorn's engineer, Frank Filipetti.

More straightforward than anything Korn had written to date, often short and sharp bursts of Nu-influenced metal were based around simple but effective riffs, punchy rhythms and strong hooks, all of which still unashamedly sounded like Korn. Davis' vocals were fiercer than ever; his death metal-like growls occasionally heard on previous releases becoming more dominant on almost every song, harsh and toxic in their deliveries. Despite the music's relative simplicity, there were still some potential classics and sure-fire fan favourites included, such as the lead single, 'Right Now', 'Did My Time', and the resurgence of the *Neidermayer's Mind* demo, 'Alive', which finally received an overhaul a decade after its original reveal. Hip-hop icon, Nas, guested on the album, and Korn even rebelled against their own management and record label with the tongue-in-cheek 'Y'All Want a Single'.

Released on 21 November 2003 and four days earlier than initially planned due to it leaking online, *Take a Look in the Mirror* debuted at 19 in America with first-week sales of just under 180,000; but when you consider this was based solely on only a few days' worth of sales and not a full week's, not to mention internet piracy become even more of a cancer to the music industry, Korn's sixth opus fared pretty well. Eventually peaking at nine on the *Billboard*

200 and going platinum within a month, it was still a satisfactory result even though Korn had been used to better.

Gaining mixed reviews but still proving popular amongst fans, *Take a Look in The Mirror* has, in the years which have passed, been named by both Davis and Welch as their least favourite Korn album. Leaving behind the child abuse themes in their artwork for the first time, an antique mirror dominates the front cover, which confirmed Davis' quote from a 2003 interview where he discussed how the album came about, 'This album is about us as a band, taking a look in the mirror and remembering where we came from, remembering our roots, going back to basics.'

'Right Now' (Korn)

Cementing Korn's original statement of taking a simplistic approach this time around, 'Right Now' kicks off with a devilish sounding riff and Arvizu's bass sounding louder than ever before, and with production not as clean and grandiose as previously experienced on *Issues* and *Untouchables*, the rough and distorted feel of *Korn* and *Life Is Peachy* is quickly brought to mind as *Take a Look in the Mirror* bursts into action. Jonathan Davis still sounds extremely pissed off with the world, quoted in a 2003 interview how 'Right Now' is based on him 'hating everyone and everything around me', ferociously screaming further into the song with the threat of 'I'm gonna fuck you up'.

A decent chorus completes a strong opening song which may not have been as explosive as 'Blind' or 'Here to Stay', but its popularity hasn't gone unnoticed by Korn, who continue to include 'Right Now' in their live setlists – the only song from the album to do so. In America, it reached 11 on *Billboard*'s Mainstream Rock Tracks chart and 13 on the Alternative Songs chart.

For the music video, an online contest was created which encouraged fans and independent directors to create a video from scratch, and in the end, Gregory Ecklund won. Using his character, Lloyd, who appears to be an impulsive and mentally ill person who likes to harm himself, the character was originally created for Spike and Mike's Sick and Twisted Festival of Animation. Producing a series of short films under the *Lloyd's Lunchbox* title, footage from the shorts were used for the 'Right Now' video, but it certainly wasn't the kind of promo Korn fans were used to seeing from their favourite band.

While the song plays, Lloyd causes plenty of self-destruction. He eats his own bogies, smashes his teeth out with a hammer, pulls his fingernails off with knives and tweezers and even shoves a pencil all the way into his ear. But the video still managed to receive heavy rotation on MTV2's *Headbanger's Ball*, while an alternative 'Mirror Mix' was directed by Nathan Cox and included on limited pressings of the *Take a Look in the Mirror* album.

'Break Some Off' (Korn)

Considered by Davis as the heaviest song Korn had produced at that point, 'Break Some Off' is a two-and-a-half-minute punisher which is led by Welch's corrosive riff. While its verses are cleaner and contain some creepy guitar tweaks, it is the rabid hook and Davis' deathly growls which make the real impact, as the frontman documents his inability to keep himself together and therefore loses control. Another bruising bout of bass work and David Silveria's mighty drum sections add further muscle, and although it is shorter in length than the majority of Korn's songs, 'Break Some Off' still slams relentlessly hard.

'Counting on Me' (Korn)

So similar in its songwriting formula, 'Counting on Me' could be considered the brother or sister to 'Thoughtless', a mid-paced and multi-layered anthem and one of the highlights of *Take a Look in the Mirror*. Heavy but with hints of melody, not to mention a huge classic Korn chorus where Davis talks of being there for someone who fails to return the favour – the lump in the throat line 'I always stay when I should leave' striking a nerve with many a listener.

An explosive bridge contains more earth-shattering screams of anguish, a catchy riff drives the song along throughout, and a double chorus closes out a track which, considering the band was in a creative lull, sounds absolutely stellar.

'Here It Comes Again' (Korn)

Perhaps the first indication Korn wasn't firing on all cylinders during the album's writing process, and considering the quality of songs to come before it, 'Here It Comes Again' is one of the weaker efforts which finds Davis screaming in frustration 'Can't I ever win?' While the verses sound decent and contain a focus on melody, an average chorus relies more on the bass and drums to fire it into life, but even Arvizu and Silveria cannot save this one. Not one of Korn's essential cuts.

'Deep Inside' (Korn)

Another largely safe number that clocks in at the three-minute mark, Davis reveals his struggles from the off by telling us he isn't doing too great. Saved by a bridge that mellows for some funk-laden moments of retrospection, as well as Silveria's continually consistent drum skills, 'Deep Inside' saunters along without ever truly igniting, and all the early momentum seems like it is getting close to being lost.

'Did My Time' (Korn)

An instant shift in both power and quality sees Korn hit form once again with a song on a whole other level to the rest of the album. A forceful droning riff is the key here, thankfully salvaged from the *Untouchables* sessions after Michael Beinhorn failed to see any potential in Shaffer's guitar creation. A sumptuous build-up of Shaffer's riff and flourishes of bass and drum spurts lead to some groovy rhythms and bouncing verses, before a phenomenal chorus and pulsating breakdown steals the limelight. Lyrically, Davis opens up about hoping his fortunes change, as he mentioned in a late 2003 interview, 'I paid my dues, I did my time, when is something good gonna happen?'

'Did My Time' was completed in early 2003 and then the band was approached by Paramount Pictures, who wanted to use the song in the movie *Lara Croft Tomb Raider: The Cradle of Life*. In the end the song was used during the movie's end credits, and its Dave Meyers-directed music video included shots from the motion picture as well as Korn performing in front of Angelina Jolie (who played Lara Croft in the movie) in a back alley. Although it couldn't be included on the official soundtrack album due to certain clauses in Jonathan Davis' contract, 'Did My Time' helped promote *Take a Look in The Mirror* even after the original hype surrounding the song had died down. Also nominated for a Best Metal Performance Grammy in 2004 (losing out to Metallica's 'St. Anger'), 'Did My Time' earned Korn their first Hot 100 entry (40), while 15 in the UK Singles chart was also considered a huge success.

'Everything I've Known' (Korn)

The final of three singles released from *Take a Look in the Mirror*, 'Everything I've Known' details a relationship gone sour, with further connotations leading an emotional reaction to what is perceived to be the decline of the music industry during the Noughties. Groove-oriented with a catchy pre-chorus and some hypnotic vocal effects, this is another strong addition to the album's track listing, even though 'Counting on Me' would have been a much better choice for a single release.

After getting the gig to direct the 'Right Now' video, Gregory Ecklund returned with another animated video which received moderate airplay. Featuring flying skeletal beings, a cyclops and figures with only teeth on their face, it was a very random and plotless short film that wasn't to live long in the memory. At the time, it was also a sign that Korn's large budgets had diminished as their popularity also appeared to be waning.

'Play Me' (Korn, Nasir bin Olu Dara Jones)

An excellent collaboration up there with Ice Cube's inclusion on 'Children of the Korn' back in 1998 sees hip-hop icon Nas, surface on a Korn song, having met the band and become pals with them a year earlier. Taking on lead vocals and rapping over Welch and Shaffer's distorted guitars as Silveria's hip-hop influenced drum rhythms return to add bounce, Nas spits venom throughout and especially on a strong hook where the use of gang vocals works well. Jonathan Davis enters the fray ahead of a brash breakdown where he delivers some more evil growls, before Nas returns for one final torrent of rap swagger.

Although Nu Metal was on the decline at this time, Nas' inclusion showed that hip-hop and metal combinations remained an appealing prospect for many artists, and while it didn't get as much exposure, 'Play Me' is still an excellent but ultimately overlooked gem.

'Alive' (Korn)

The song from which the whole of *Take a Look in the Mirror* was based, and certainly sounding like it was born much earlier than in 2003, Korn finally decided to bring 'Alive' out of the doldrums – having been lying dormant since the band's *Neidermayer's Mind* demo a decade prior.

The chorus melody was taken back from 'Need To', which amusingly led to some of the less hardcore Korn fans branding 'Alive' a rehash – not realising that 'Need To' had in fact done the same thing. Arvizu's raw bass opening and another coarse riff takes us back to 1994, but this time, Jonathan Davis takes his rightful place on the mic as opposed to Welch, who sang on the original version. Pulsating and the epitome of Korn's back to basics approach on album number six, 'Alive' is another highlight and its long-awaited inclusion appears completely justified.

'Let's Do This Now' (Korn)

Davis' bagpipes make a quick cameo for a short intro blast before they make way for a dominating riff which is backed up by more overpowering bass work from Arvizu. There is a slight cinematic feel to a chorus where high note rhythms are prominent, and Davis' mix of clean and harsh vocals continue in the same trend as much of the album. Returning to safe territory, 'Let's Do This Now' is a standard album track that lacks somewhat of a bite.

'I'm Done' (Korn)

Fusing elements from both *Issues* and *Untouchables*, 'I'm Done' immediately brings 'Falling Away from Me' to mind with its atmospheric and tension-filled opening. Softer verses offer a change in formula, and what you think to be the pre-chorus actually reveals itself to be the main hook. A nice surprise to separate itself from the rest of the pack, Korn at least show a few hints of experimentation instead of completely settling on revisiting their early sound. Lyrically, Davis has finally had enough of being used ('I'm done being there for others, they have their pain and so do I'), and while the song doesn't get as much attention as many of the band's others, 'I'm Done' certainly touched a few fans' hearts upon first listen.

'Y'All Want a Single' (Korn)

Korn raised a collective middle finger to both their own record label and their management with this one, written in response to their bosses wanting the band to write a hit single. Containing 89 uses of the word 'Fuck', musically this is a lively rocker containing decent yet simplistic riffs, thumping bass lines and animated drumming, while its chorus is delivered through Davis' hostile barking but in somewhat of a singalong fashion. Shaffer said in a 2003 interview:

> For the first time in our lives, we were dissecting our music and trying to analyse the structure of those songs ('Got the Life' and 'Freak on a Leash'),

trying to figure out what made them huge hits. But Korn never works like that, and while we were wondering, Jonathan came up with the line 'Y'All want a single, say: FUCK THAT!' and we wrote that song as a big fuck you to them (Epic Records).

It was never going to be a hit, but it was still released as a single, the radio edit laughably replacing 'Fuck' with 'Suck'. In the accompanying music video, directed by Andrews Jenkins, 30 statements criticising record labels and the music industry flash across the screen while Korn and some of their fans smash up a record store. Among the truth bombs, such statements as 'The record company wanted to change this video. We didn't.' and 'Britney Spears' last video cost $1,000,000. This Korn video costs $150,000.' are seen; and a lot of the facts shown are still relevant to the industry today. Clearly not worried about any potential reprisals for their antics, perhaps in part due to the fact their record deal with Epic was coming to an end, Korn continued to do things their own way and 'Y'All Want a Single' was exactly the result they were looking for.

'When Will This End' (Korn)

The weakest closing track of any of the first six albums, 'When Will This End' trudges along with a *Life Is Peachy* vibe. Downbeat riffs and a thrash-tinged drum flurry cement themselves on a mid-paced number where you get the feeling that Korn had finally hit a brick wall. Unlike previous closers, there is no epic finale here, just the sense of an album track that may have been better placed somewhere midway through. 'Y'All Want a Single' would have been a much better way to put a full stop to the record, but alas, all ends not so well before six minutes of silence follows.

'One' (James Hetfield, Lars Ulrich)

Having been recorded during their performance at MTV Icon: Metallica in May 2003, Korn's cover of the thrash metal legends' anti-war song which featured on their 1988 album ...*And Justice for All* is a glorious tribute to one of the biggest metal bands there has ever been. A few minutes shorter than the original but nonetheless captivating, even the iconic guitar solo is expertly performed and well received. There are videos online of Korn's performance which earned them a standing ovation from all four members of Metallica, and this live recording makes 'One' a worthy hidden track to finish off *Take a Look in The Mirror* on a much brighter note than 'When Will This End' did.

See You on the Other Side (2005)

Personnel:
Jonathan Davis: vocals, bagpipes
James 'Munky' Shaffer: lead and rhythm guitars
Reginald 'Fieldy' Arvizu: bass guitar
David Silveria: drums
Record label: Virgin
Recorded at: Jonathan Davis' home studio, Los Angeles, California, USA, June-November 2005
Produced by: Jonathan Davis, The Matrix, Atticus Ross
Release date: 6 December 2005
Highest chart positions: US: 3, UK: 71
Running time: 61:01

As Korn were set to begin work on their seventh album, the metal world was left stunned when Brian 'Head' Welch quit the band. With his addiction to meth spiralling further out of control, and on top of that a heavy reliance on alcohol, Xanax and sleeping pills; not to mention having a young daughter to care for, Welch found God and became a born-again Christian. In his 2007 book, *Save Me from Myself,* Welch revealed that he walked away from his band via an email, initially saying he didn't want to tour anymore. In response, Jonathan Davis offered to bring in a replacement guitarist for live shows, so long as Welch stayed on to record what would become *See You on the Other Side,* but after taking direction from his newfound beliefs, Welch cut all ties and his departure from Korn was officially announced by the band's management on 22 February 2005. Shaffer reminisced on Welch's departure in 2016 when speaking to *Metal Hammer,* 'I was sitting alone in a big house, I was going through a bad time myself, and I just couldn't believe it. I was in disbelief for weeks and I was devastated.'

Welch's departure was one of many changes for Korn. After releasing their *Greatest Hits Vol. 1* compilation at the back end of 2004, the now-quartet left their Epic/Immortal label and signed to Virgin Records while also partnering with EMI. As part of an innovative and highly lucrative deal for the band, Virgin paid Korn $25 million in exchange for some of the profits of their next two albums, as well as from tours and merchandise sales – two areas previously off-limits to record companies. Virgin also received a 30% stake in the band's licensing, ticket sales and further sources of revenue, which to the naked eye seemed a win-win for Korn and an extremely brave move for their new record label.

Recorded and produced in Jonathan Davis' home studio, Korn also enlisted the renowned production team, The Matrix. Consisting of Lauren Christy, Graham Edwards and Scott Spock, and having previously only worked with pop acts such as Britney Spears and Shakira, The Matrix also earned songwriting credits as once again, Korn treaded new and leftfield waters. English musician and composer Atticus Ross was also involved in programming.

Released on 6 December 2005, *See You on the Other Side* was a highly experimental affair that contained elements of industrial rock, gothic rock, and new wave; and featured strong uses of synth and electronics. Receiving better reviews than previous effort, *Take a Look in the Mirror*, Korn's seventh opus still shifted 220,000 copies in the US in its first week of release, with a lot of people seeming interested in hearing how Korn would sound with James 'Munky' Shaffer taking on the role of sole guitarist. Debuting at 3 in America and 71 in the UK, Korn's homeland certainly showed more support than anywhere else, but with Nu Metal losing its mainstream power and a new wave of modern metal bands taking over, Korn suddenly took a back seat to the likes of Lamb Of God, Killswitch Engage, Trivium and Five Finger Death Punch. Regardless, *See You on the Other Side* went gold within a month and by mid-March 2006, it had been certified platinum.

As part of a ten-month promotional tour, Korn brought back Family Values for the first time since 2001, where Deftones co-headlined and their frontman, Chino Moreno, regularly joined Korn on stage to perform their rendition of Ice Cube's 'Wicked', which had previously been included on *Life Is Peachy*. A second stage on the Family Values tour showcased up-and-coming acts, where Walls of Jericho, Bury Your Dead and Droid, amongst others, were popular additions. An estimated 400,000 people turned out for the 30-date run, and further tours in the US, Europe and Asia saw Mudvayne, 10 Years, Disturbed, Hatebreed, Flyleaf and Soulfly play supporting roles on selected dates.

Korn hired the surrealist and gothic artist, David Stoupakis, to create the artwork for *See You on the Other Side*. Giving him a line from the album track, 'Seen It All', Stoupakis created an image which depicts a teary-eyed young boy holding a headless teddy bear, as behind him stood human torsos with rabbit and horse heads. Stormy skies are in the background and, although not as dark as previous covers, this one still had a nightmarish and unsettling feel to it which wasn't necessarily in keeping with some of the music on show.

'Twisted Transistor' (Korn, The Matrix)

The first insight into a four-piece Korn, 'Twisted Transistor' found the band free of their heavy and uncompromising sound as this pop-tinged rocker leads off with Shaffer's simplistic guitar chords and David Silveria's electronically charged drumming. Arvizu's instantly recognisable bass work is no more, as the click and crunch he so famously creates has been removed to make way for a cleaner undercurrent, and Jonathan Davis' vocals are also purer and less forceful.

With all that being said, this is still a rousing opening, and while it isn't the Korn that people had become accustomed to, 'Twisted Transistor' is an extremely catchy song with an irresistible hook. Focusing on the power music has in making you feel good no matter how bad things get in your life, the lead single from *See You on the Other Side* reached 64 on *Billboard*'s Hot 100 and 27 in the UK Singles chart, as a Head-less Korn flew out of the gates with plenty of fighting spirit.

Continuing their tongue-in-cheek videos, Korn went Spinal Tap on a mockumentary of sorts for 'Twisted Transistor'. Directed by Ryan Ratajski and starring Lil Jon as Davis, Snoop Dogg as Shaffer, Xzibit as Arvizu and David Banner as Silveria, the hip-hoppers play in a small seedy club, take on signing sessions, commit rock star antics on a tour bus and party like it is 1999. Banner's modelling scene is funny due to its correlation with Silveria's early modelling career, and Snoop Dogg takes the spotlight by suggesting Shaffer is a hostile character with severe anger issues- which is the exact opposite of the guitarist's true nature. The real Korn have a cameo at the end as they portray themselves as representatives from the record label, 'Fony Records', and despite its outrageous treatment, the video was very much a hit.

'Politics' (Korn, The Matrix)

'I'm political to a point where it affects human life,' Davis told MTV News in 2005, 'from global warming to abortion to my gun rights. Those are the kind of politics that I care about.' Building the momentum which 'Twisted Transistor' started, 'Politics' is another energetic and appealing song containing vibrant guitar work and uplifting drum sections. Passionately delivered are Davis' vocal leads where he openly says he doesn't give a shit about politics, and a feisty chorus is driven by electronic swathes which nicely accompany Shaffer's guitar playing.

Chosen to be the third single from the album, although it didn't really bother the charts, 'Politics' is another standout moment on an album which many feared could spell the end for the nu metal heroes; but early on, things are looking very positive.

While Korn were on their Family Values tour in 2006, they decided to film a music video for 'Politics' with the help of some of their fans. As well as traditional camera footage coming from Chris Kantrowitz, the band gave ten lucky fan club members all-access passes and handheld cameras to shoot performance and behind the scenes footage at the Alpine Valley Amphitheatre show in East Troy, Wisconsin, and the finished product was exclusively released on MP3.com on October 3, 2006.

'Hypocrites' (Korn, The Matrix)

Due to some animosity between Davis and Welch after the guitarist left Korn, some were left wondering whether parting shots might be fired by the band at their awakened former bandmate, and while certain lyrics on *See You on the Other Side* could be seen to have such meaning, 'Hypocrites' has to contain some of the most obvious examples.

Written by Davis about his 'total disgust for Christianity', where he takes shots at organised religion and talks about how church leaders get rich by taking contributions from their followers, the scathing line of 'Your messiah was never mine' is perhaps the starkest instant where his frustration boils over.

Musically, 'Hypocrites' is darker and heavier than what has come before it, and it is steeped in electronics. Vocally, Davis comes over with a certain degree of aggression. Mid-paced and experimental, while the song may not feature one of the band's bolder choruses, it certainly makes its presence, and Korn's intentions, known from the outset.

'Souvenir' (Korn, The Matrix, Atticus Ross)

Opening with a gloriously distorted riff and some of the heaviest instrumentation thus far, 'Souvenir' finds Davis returning to his high school bullies for another backlash, as he once again stands above them and reminds them of where he is now. The angst isn't there anymore, though; in fact, as a listener who has travelled Korn's journey from the early days, it almost sounds as if the frontman has finally come to terms with what happened and is in a forgiving mood, battle-hardened after he has fought much tougher fights since and still come out the other side.

Industrial-sounding with a middle section dominated by electronics, there is even a bout of rap vocals thrown in for good measure, as well as a decent chorus; and while 'Souvenir' isn't one of the most explosive moments on the album, it is perhaps one of the most satisfying in terms of proving you can always overcome life's toughest of obstacles.

'10 or a 2-Way' (Korn, The Matrix, Atticus Ross)

Showing that Jonathan Davis still has a deviant side to him, '10 or a 2-Way' appears to look at prostitutes and women who are only after one thing. Sexually provocative lyrics, including the lines 'When you cum (be a good girl), hold your breath (make it last long)', and 'Only fucking you till the seasons change' are backed up by rasping guitars, boisterous drum sections, and an oversaturation of murky electronics.

A standard album track and nothing more, the first skit/interlude follows the song's culmination where Davis dusts off his bagpipes, mixing the recording of them being played to sound faster and obscure. Strange like all the skits which would follow, a deep breathing that sounds like Darth Vader from *Star Wars* follows the bagpipes before, thankfully, this rather pointless inclusion comes to a close.

'Throw Me Away' (Korn, The Matrix, Atticus Ross)

A line used many times during a Korn song in the past, and with lyrical content finding Davis begging for help and salvation, 'Throw Me Away' is somewhat of a ballad that is smothered in Gothicism. Squelchy synth and darkened ambience make this sound more like a Nine Inch Nails track, where slow and spooky verses are redundant of guitar and bass. It is interesting to hear Korn take on something like this, and while it might be a love it or hate it kind of song, 'Throw Me Away' is a fine addition that continues to keep the band's vision evolving.

'Love Song' (Korn, The Matrix, Atticus Ross)

Not what the song title suggests, 'Love Song' hints at Davis talking about his mother ('Son of a man you loved and left for, the son of a bitch who tried to show me death's door'); however, some also perceived the track to be aimed at Welch due to later lines hinting at religious implications. Compared to other songs on *See You on the Other Side*, Davis does sound much more antagonistic here, and while Silveria's electronic drums still take some getting used to and meaty distortion drowns out any force that Shaffer's guitar work may possess, 'Love Song' is another safe listen which lacks any real significance.

'Open Up' (Korn, The Matrix, Atticus Ross)

A drug ballad in which Korn start to regain their footing, 'Open Up' sees Arvizu's clicking bass lines make a welcome return, as they lead a bouncing verse that still has electronics outweighing guitar power. With a hook so strong that it doesn't need meaty instrumentation, the impact of 'Open Up' is fine the way it is, as Davis' chorus line of 'You're corrupted by some sick fuck' once again questions if Welch, and God, are the targets of his potent lyricism.

A small string section is a nice addition during a middle section of calm, and a final chorus with some effective backing vocals finds Korn returning to form. A sombre skit follows with an acoustic guitar cameo, bagpipes and a hip-hop beat, and some of Davis' babble vocals hark back to *Issues*-era Korn.

'Coming Undone' (Korn, The Matrix)

And so the heaviness returns with a simple but now well-loved lead riff on a track that has become a huge fan favourite. 'Guess the black thoughts have come again to get me', says a resigned Davis on this bulky rocker, where the clap of the electronic drums reverberates throughout. In some ways, it is hard to see why so many people jumped on board with 'Coming Undone' in the sense that it is not your typical Korn anthem. There is no bombastic chorus or ferocious bridge, Davis' vocals are strong, but he never has to break his stride; and Arvizu's bass work is once again buried deep under. Still, the song received strong plaudits and it became a shoo-in on future live setlists for many years to come. Towards the end, Davis lets us all know he is still human with the line of 'Looks like I'm getting better'. A surprise success.

Directed by the then-known Little X (now known as Director X and real name Julien Christian Lutz), the music video for 'Coming Undone' finds Korn performing in a vast desert in broad daylight. As the performance progresses, the sky begins to crack and reveal the night sky, which in turn cracks and shatters to make way for nothing but white. By the end, the band members have all unravelled to nothingness, literally coming undone, if you will, for a decent but unspectacular promo flick.

'Getting Off' (Korn, The Matrix)

Musically decent where the guitars and drums rise up to make this another one of the heavier songs on *See You on the Other Side*, 'Getting Off' is let down by more naughty and immature lyrics about, ahem, masturbation. 'Hold my knees, lick my treat, I'm coming on you!' tells you all you need to know about Jonathan Davis' mind space when he wrote this one, and with its repetitive and underwhelming chorus on top, 'Getting Off' is more filler than killer, and not quite the climax you hope for.

'Liar' (Korn, The Matrix)

A full-on Korn anthem with more scathing lyrics which can either be taken about a woman who controls her partner, or a religious trashing amid Welch's recent conversion, 'Liar' is a beast of a song. Led by a dominating riff and David Silveria's best drum performance on the whole album, Davis also brings his scat vocal out of the closet on a pulsating bridge. A grinding chorus hits the spot, and a few more songs like this would surely have given *See You on the Other Side* a far more formidable standing within Korn's back catalogue.

Another interlude brings back the bagpipes, as well as some strong guitar effects and turntable scratching, but even though these inclusions are frequent, they continue to feel out of place and unimportant in the grand scheme of things.

Perhaps not considered a favourite music video due to it not even being included on the band's YouTube channel, the animated Tony Shiff-produced promo for 'Liar' finds Korn performing on the face of a clock tower. The graphics reek of the video games of the early to mid-2000s, and despite having almost a decade on 'Freak on a Leash', the animation seen here is nowhere near as impressive as that of Todd McFarlane and his team, back in 1998. Shiff began creating such videos for an MTV2 series called *Video Mods*, and 'Liar' was due to be part of a series on Yahoo! Music called *Artist Mods*, but when Yahoo! lost its sponsorship, the video was unable to be uploaded in time. Vimeo appears to be one of the only platforms this video can be viewed on these days, and so it is not surprising that many Korn fans still don't know it exists.

'For No One' (Korn, The Matrix)

Aimed at the band's doubters and also authority in general, 'For No One' has a late 1990s feel with its powerful intro. Shaffer's downbeat riff sounds huge, as does some thrash-tinged drumming, and Arvizu lets loose with some of his classic groovy bass work. A rousing chorus is delivered with verve, bringing the best parts of the now-defunct nu metal movement to mind for a belated but much-needed swansong. Heavy but catchy as hell, 'For No One' reminds us that Korn can still run with the best of them, even if these high points were more sporadic during the band's toughest of times.

'Seen It All' (Korn, The Matrix, Atticus Ross)

One of the most experimental moments on the album which brings back some industrial elements and another comparison to Nine Inch Nails, an eerie and sauntering opening includes some creepy electronics before Davis takes over with frustration as he opens himself up and revisits the years since Korn began. Talking about being called 'an animal', 'a victim', 'a witness on the witch-hunt' and 'the voice that's in your head', 'Seen It All' is an apt title for a song which documents a been there, done that, got the t-shirt kind of story.

Symphonic backings add further drama and melancholy at certain points, but the overall industrial crunch leaves the most lasting impression. The song from which David Stoupakis was given a line in order to create the album's artwork, 'Seen It All', has added importance and lives long in the memory for many reasons.

'Tearjerker' (Korn, The Matrix, Atticus Ross, Leo Ross)

A dark and demented ballad of sorts finds Davis stripping his soul bare one more time. Early on, 'Tearjerker' is just the frontman and some dystopian electronics, his delicate vocals reeking of emotion as he reveals how he wished there was someone to love him. A haunting number picks up in both pace and volume later on, where some fuzzy guitars and one more bout of expert powerhouse drumming resonate over a frankly incredible Davis roar, which he delivers with both pain and passion.

Bringing The Cure to mind with some melancholic textures, 'Tearjerker' is a different kind of album closer for Korn, but it is still an engrossing and overly triumphant way to round off the band's seventh album, which just about does enough to reassure fans that a Korn without Brian Welch is still a good Korn.

'It's Me Again' (Korn, The Matrix)

The first of seven B-sides from the *See You on the Other Side* sessions, 'It's Me Again' is one of three to be included on a special edition bonus CD, and it really should have made the original track listing. Shaffer is at his potent best with some meaty guitar work, Silveria brings some crunching drum sections, and a strong chorus makes this a great addition to Korn's discography. Less reliant on electronics in favour of a guitar-driven stomp, Davis welcomes everyone back to the show with the clinical line of 'You see beauty I see pain, you see sky and I see acid rain'. Quite how this one didn't make the cut is anyone's guess, because 'It's Me Again' is up there with the band's best songs.

'Eaten Up Inside' (Korn, The Matrix)

Slightly similar to 'Coming Undone' and another song that makes a strong case for being included on the original release, 'Eaten Up Inside' is well constructed and makes an impact with more riff heaviness and counteractive drum flurries. Some prominent synth adds a nice layer, and Davis remains pained with the heart-wrenching line of 'Sick of being alive, let me die, I never got what I wanted, never got what I needed'. Packing quality and strong songwriting, this is another example of Korn rising up and showing they still have plenty left in the tank.

'Last Legal Drug (Le Petit Mort)' (Korn, The Matrix, Atticus Ross)

The last of the three bonus CD tracks, while generally dominated by industrial swathes, 'Last Legal Drug' has an intro and verse riff which sounds very much like the one used on 'Thoughtless' from *Untouchables*. The electric drum beat rarely changes throughout, neither does the mid-paced formula and with Davis going gothic and sounding like Marilyn Manson on some sinister verses drenched in melodrama, this is a decent song which is perhaps a little overlong at the five-minute mark. 'Love might be the last legal drug' is a prominent and all too true lyric, but it thrives on a song that emphasises Korn's experimental ventures as of late.

'Inside Out' (Korn, The Matrix)

A bonus track on the special edition iTunes release, 'Inside Out' is a light-hearted love song of sorts in which Davis talks about wanting a woman at any costs – ugly or not. 'I'd drink the milk that's in your breast, I wouldn't even mind your shit' he confidently protests, on one of the three verses, which are led by 1980s-sounding pop-tinged harmonies. A heavy chorus and an abrasive bridge ramp up the volume, but this is another song in Korn's repertoire which cannot be taken too seriously. Most definitely deserving of B-side status at best.

'Too Late I'm Dead' (Korn, The Matrix)

An addition to the Japanese release of *See You on the Other Side*, 'Too Late I'm Dead' opens with an effective trap beat and small flourishes of bass guitar funk. Davis whispers away on gloomy verses before he fires up his pipes on a frenzied and rampaging chorus and, littered with dark and twisted grooves whilst containing further emphasis on industrial nuances, this is a decent outing as Korn showed somewhat of a creative peak in 2005.

'Appears' (Korn, The Matrix)

Regularly showing up on YouTube but never officially released, 'Appears' might not be a particularly affluent Korn track, but fans who have come across it certainly took it to their hearts. Shaffer's hardened riffs sound good and the pristine production allows Silveria's drumming to stand out, but this mid-paced rocker finds a weaker Davis trudging through without his usually clinical edge. 'It's only ever violence that's in my touch, appears I am built this way' he sings on a below-par chorus.

'I'm the One' (Korn, The Matrix)

There is something special about this final B-side, which also never had an official release. In many ways, 'I'm the One' is more of a prolonged intro/

Above: Ready to lay waste once again. (*Sebastien Paquet*)

Below: The red mist descends – a 2019 promo photo. (*Edigwiki*)

Left: A not so immaculate inception, but Korn were braced for battle with their *Neidermayer's Mind* demo in 1993. *(Korn)*

Right: Sinister beginnings as Korn made a visual impact as well as an audible one with their debut full-length in 1994. *(Epic)*

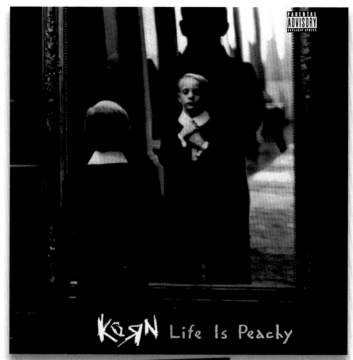

Right: Another nightmare unfolds with *Life Is Peachy* in 1996. (*Epic*)

Left: Todd McFarlane's now iconic cover design for *Follow the Leader*, Korn's first number one album. (*Epic*)

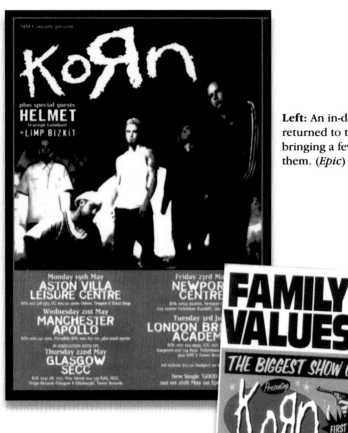

Left: An in-demand Korn returned to the UK in 1997, bringing a few friends along with them. (*Epic*)

Right: The first-ever *Family Values Tour* launched with this eye-catching line-up and poster. (*Epic*)

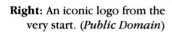

Right: An iconic logo from the very start. (*Public Domain*)

Left: James 'Munky' Shaffer dressed to impress on Live on the *Other Side* DVD. (*Epic*)

Right: Brian Welch doing what he does best with a 7-string guitar. (*Josie Borisow*)

Left: The debut of the now synonymous Korn related ragdoll, created by Alfredo Carlos for the front cover of *Issues*. (*Epic*)

Right: The winning and runner-up designs in the MTV competition for the cover art of Issues. (*Epic*)

Right: Costing over $4 million to create, *Untouchables* is huge in sound and grandiose in its delivery. (*Epic*)

Left: The last album to feature the original line-up, *Take a Look in the Mirror's* rawness saw Korn going back to basics. (*Epic*)

Left: Jonathan Davis – a formidable frontman. (*Pistenwolf*)

Right: Regi 'Fieldy' Arvizu with his bass, rattle and roll. (*Pitpony Photography*)

Left: People say he Munky's around... (*Nash84*)

Right: All out action when Korn supplied 'Did My Time' to the 2003 *Tomb Raider* movie. (*Epic*)

Left: A 'Head'-less Korn at the MTV Asia Awards in 2006. (*Sry85*)

Left: The nightmare continued as a four-piece Korn emerged to prove their doubters wrong, with *See You on the Other Side* in 2005. (*Virgin*)

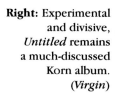

Right: Experimental and divisive, *Untitled* remains a much-discussed Korn album. (*Virgin*)

Right: Returning to their roots and Ross Robinson for *Korn III* in 2010. (*Roadrunner*)

Left: Metal meets dubstep and drum and bass as *The Path of Totality* instantly divided Korn's fans. (*Roadrunner*)

Left: Davis and his custom-made mic stand which he calls 'The Bitch'. (*Stefan Krause*)

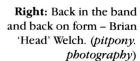

Right: Back in the band and back on form – Brian 'Head' Welch. (*pitpony. photography*)

Left: Ray Luzier quickly felt at home in Korn's line-up. (*Alexandre Cardoso*)

Right: Korn in the live environment. (*Steven Lek*)

Left: Shaffer like an axe-man possessed. (*Sven Mandel*)

Right: Regi with his visually funky bass. (*Antje Naumann*)

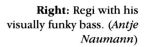

Left: With Welch back in the fold, *The Paradigm Shift* began Korn's journey back to the top. (*Universal*)

Right: Irresistably heavy – *The Serenity of Suffering* found Korn back to their best in 2016. (*Roadrunner*)

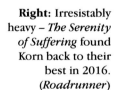

Right: An album born out of grief, an album to rival Korn's greatest releases – the emotional rollercoaster that is *The Nothing*. (*Roadrunner*)

Left: The Jonathan Davis-inspired soundtrack for the vampire chiller, *Queen of the Damned*. (*Warner*)

Left: Like old times – Korn and Limp Bizkit co-headline a UK Tour in 2016. (*Roadrunner*)

Right: Hell arose when Korn and Slipknot joined forces for the UK's tour of the year in 2015. (*Roadrunner*)

outro than an actual song, but it is dark, eerie, gothic and outlandish. Haunting strings play a prominent role as they back up Davis' delicate whispering, while intense but smothered drums echo and add to the unsettling atmosphere. 'I'm the one looking down on you, where do you go when no one's there' says a provocative frontman, who in this instance sounds just as impactful as on Korn's greatest numbers.

Untitled (2007)

Personnel:
Jonathan Davis: vocals, bagpipes, drums
James 'Munky' Shaffer: lead and rhythm guitars
Reginald 'Fieldy' Arvizu: bass guitar
Terry Bozzio: drums
Brooks Wackerman: drums
Zac Baird: keyboards, organ, synthesiser
Record label: Virgin
Recorded at: Jonathan Davis' studio, Los Angeles, California, USA, late 2006-early 2007
Produced by: Korn, The Matrix, Atticus Ross
Release date: 31 July 2007
Highest chart positions: US: 2, UK: 15
Running time: 48:47

After *See You on the Other Side* found Korn adapting to life as a four-piece, another spanner was thrown into the works when in December 2006, at the end of the end of the band's current tour cycle, it was announced that David Silveria was stepping away from his drum kit and going on a hiatus. Choosing to spend time with his family, as well as focusing on his sushi and grill restaurant in Huntington Beach (later turning it into a rock and sports bar), it soon became apparent to the remaining trio that Silveria would not be returning to the band ahead of the writing and recording of their next album.

In the years which followed, Silveria became outspoken about his former bandmates and cut all ties with them after claiming he wasn't allowed to return after his extended absence. In 2015, he sued the band for money he believed he was owed from the previous nine years, leading to Jonathan Davis saying on Twitter that he would 'never, never' play with Silveria again. Since departing Korn, the drummer has embarked on a handful of new music projects – Infinika in 2014, the very brief Core 10 in 2018, and currently, he is back behind the kit with the alternative metal band, Breaking In A Sequence.

To complete the second of their two-album deal with Virgin/EMI, Korn enlisted both Terry Bozzio and Brooks Wackerman to fill the vacant drum position, while Davis himself also performed the sticks on a handful of tracks. Primarily known for his time playing with Frank Zappa, Bozzio earned strong plaudits from his temporary bandmates, so much so that Davis was even quoted as calling him 'the world's greatest drummer'. Providing a different style but successful in what he was required to do, Wackerman used his experiences of playing in the legendary crossover punks, Suicidal Tendencies, and punk rock heroes, Bad Religion, to contribute precise percussion on the tracks he was asked to perform on.

Originally due to be produced by The Matrix once again, Korn grew dissatisfied with how the production team was making the new material sound.

Deciding to part company, Atticus Ross came in and re-recorded much of what had already been done, and the results were there for all to see when on 31 July 2007, Korn's eighth studio album was released. Most commonly known as Untitled, due to the band leaving it up to the fans to name it whatever they liked, it was even more experimental than *See You on the Other Side*. Dominated by the murky keyboards of new official member Zac Baird, along with toying arrangements and progressive music, which was less free-flowing than what everyone was used to hearing from Korn, *Untitled* certainly proved to be a divisive record amongst fans and critics.

Despite its leftfield approach, there was still enough interest to guide *Untitled* to number 2 on the *Billboard* 200, with opening week sales of just over 120,000. Its early success was to be short-lived, however, as the album would completely fall off the chart within twelve weeks, and *Untitled* would become Korn's first studio album not to reach platinum status. It did go gold, though, but only just.

Steering away from the child abuse themes on their previous cover arts, Korn hired UK-born visual artist, Richard A. Kirk, to come up with something different for *Untitled's* front sleeve. Exploring the liminal space between imagination and reality and relating it to one of Kirk's main interests, the morphology of plants and animals, Kirk created a spectacular image that depicted a human body with the head of a crow. With the body symbolising a source of ideas formed into music, and the crow's head being the outlet from which the music is presented, it was perhaps fitting that this artwork (and further drawings from Kirk included in the album's booklet) cemented Korn's intention of using as much experimentation as possible on their latest record.

Ahead of the album's release, Korn announced the latest instalment of the Family Values tour, where the line-up also included gothic rock sensations Evanescence, metalcore favourites Atreyu, and the heavy metal supergroup Hellyeah, who included Mudvayne's Chad Gray and Pantera drum legend, Vinnie Paul amongst their ranks. Having offended the band after demanding a full-time slot as well as receiving 25% interest, Terry Bozzio was removed from his duties with Korn and he was replaced by Slipknot's Joey Jordison, who also filled in on the latter Bitch We Have a Problem tour.

'Intro' (Korn)
A creepy and dramatic instrumental kicks things off, which sounds like something Tim Burton could have created. A carnival-like fantasy arrangement where organs and synth play a strong role, Terry Bozzio debuts with some subtle drum swipes and Jonathan Davis provides some background howling. Unusual but intriguing, although slightly overlong at almost two minutes in length.

'Starting Over' (Korn)
The first song on the album which is lyrically inspired by Davis' June 2006 diagnosis of Immune Thrombocytopenic Purpura (ITP), a disorder in which

a low blood-platelet count prohibits the blood from clotting as it should, 'Starting Over' is a progressive rocker which is dominated by Bozzio's live-sounding drum arrangements. 'His drum kit was huge and all the colours and sounds he made pushed our music in different directions we might never have thought about going', said Davis in a 2007 interview.

As with many of the tracks on *Untitled*, this is a mid-paced but cerebral number where droning electronics overtake the effectiveness of Shaffer's downbeat riffing. Arvizu's bass work is also hidden deeper below, yet with Davis' vocals still sounding as strong as ever, this is still undeniably Korn. 'Happiness is boring, need pain instead' broods the frontman as he contemplates his near-death experience from the previous year, which he also spoke about to *Real Detroit Weekly* when promoting the album, 'It made me re-arrange my priorities in life and think about what's really important'.

Not the kind of song to instantly win over fans who may have already had reservations over the direction of *Untitled*, 'Starting Over' is saved by a stunning second-half full of haunting keys, reflective melodies, and soaring instrumentation. Davis' anguished cries of 'come take me' indicate his fear upon his initial hospitalisation, the emotion seeping out on a song which ends on the highest of notes.

'Bitch We Got a Problem' (Korn)

On a song which details schizophrenia, the tempo picks up even though Korn choose to lead with dirty low-end synth. Some decent guitar leads dip in and out, but distortion is the order of the day. Davis pulls double duty on 'Bitch We Got a Problem', as he takes on the drum work and presents simple but lively patterns, while his vocals include frantic bouts which are relevant to the subject matter at hand, 'Real close to schizophrenic I fear, say how many voices you hear' he spouts at one point. It is also worth noting the song title has been used within Korn's lyrics before, having appeared in 'Getting Off' on *See You on the Other Side*, where on that occasion it had a whole other futile meaning.

'Evolution' (Korn)

Brooks Wackerman debuts on the album's lead single, which is an upbeat number with a more accessible feel to the rest of the track listing. Shaffer's guitar work takes the lead at last, and it is supported by some spongy synth and peculiar electronics, and a strong chorus that is straight to the point is probably the best of the whole album.

Studying the concept of humans regressing and destroying their environment while other species advance and adapt to their conditions, a bizarre theme is taken on which, although serious, was hard to be taken as such by many upon hearing of Korn's intentions for 'Evolution'. To promote the song, Korn set up the web domain evolutiondevolution.com, where the theme circled around a documentary site and the band members acted as experts who studied evolution for a fake documentary titled Devolution: Nature's U-Turn. In doing this, Korn's idea caused some controversy when the new wave band, Devo, called Korn imposters. Devo's bassist, Gerald Casale, argued that his band were the pioneers of the concept of devolution, from which their own name had originated, however, the argument was nothing more than a storm in a teacup.

'Evolution' reached four on *Billboard*'s Mainstream Rock Songs chart, and a vicious breakdown midway through the song put Wackerman's drumming talents on show for the first time, while clearly identifying a different style to Terry Bozzio, which was still just as engrossing.

In keeping with the song's theme, a Dave Meyers-directed music video also made for interesting viewing. According to the casting call sheet, the video was listed as being filled with political satire and humour, and predominantly male actors were sought to fill roles of scientists, religious politicians, doctors, anthropologists, and military men. Korn perform in front of charts which show IQ decline in humans, going further to confirm the human race to be in a poor state. An 'Evolution Crisis Summit' later compares humans to monkeys, proving our race to be in peril when a scantily clad woman offers a monkey the choice of a wad of cash, or a banana, and the monkey chooses the banana. Due to not having an official drummer at that point, Slipknot's Joey Jordison can be seen performing on the kit in the video.

'Hold On' (Korn)
Described by Shaffer as 'The closest thing to an original Korn song' on the album, 'Hold On' is a rousing track that is guitar-driven and packs a forceful punch. Arvizu's bass work is given the chance to shine, Wackerman's drumming is well constructed, and Davis sounds like the frontman of old who once again documents his fight with ITP. Called a 'song of empowerment', the line of 'Hold on, be strong' attests to that statement perfectly. Had there been a few more straight-up rockers such as this, then perhaps *Untitled* would have fared better, but maybe that is why 'Hold On' stands out from the crowd.

A funny music video accompanied the single release, where Davis and Shaffer enter a bull-riding contest, of all things – the term 'Hold On' being used in a much different context. The video was directed by Vikram Gandhi and dedicated to professional rodeo cowboy, Lane Frost, who died in 1989 from injuries sustained after dismounting a bull. With the aim to stay on the bull for eight seconds, Shaffer beats Davis to the prize – a cheque. However, Davis steals the cheque and makes a run for it through the ring, only to then be struck by a bull as the video fades to black.

'Kiss' (Korn)
Halting the momentum created by 'Evolution' and 'Hold On', Korn enter ballad territory on 'Kiss', where Zac Baird takes the reins with his keyboard skills. Bozzio gets back behind the drum kit and at times, he delivers some heavy drum patterns, while violins add a soothing texture to the emotional atmosphere. Davis longs for an ex-lover who doesn't feel the same way for him

anymore, 'I don't understand why you always push me away' he sings while also working overtime by providing some additional percussion.

'Do What They Say' (Korn)

With tensions still running high in the aftermath of Welch's departure and his allegiance to Christ, Davis appears to aim his frustrations towards religion and the effort which goes into trying to convert non-believers. 'Do what they say or they take it away, I'd rather be dead than carry on' he snarls on a biting chorus line, launched over a rich blast of synth and keys which sound like an air raid alarm. Some heavy stop-start riffs add some rawness, and Bozzio's drum sections risk devilment, leading up to a two-song salvo where Korn let loose on their former guitarist.

'Ever Be' (Korn)

'You're all that's wrong with your dumbass psalm', says Davis with intent, on a song which for many remains a tough listen due to who it is aimed at. A heavy bridge finds Bozzio delivering some powerful speed drumming, as Shaffer contributes some classic down and distorted guitar riffs. A melodic swathe of synth makes the chorus that little bit more emphatic, and the attack on Welch doesn't appear to end there...

'Love & Luxury' (Korn)

If anything, 'Love & Luxury' is a more direct call out, especially from the opening moments where Davis mutters, 'I read your little book...' By now, Welch had released his *Save Me from Myself* memoir and some of its content appeared to upset Korn's vocalist, especially. Musically, this is a very different Korn, where pop-punk guitars and a slight 1980s new wave feel leads a light-hearted number. The chorus is catchy even if you get the feeling it isn't meant to be taken too seriously, in fact, had Welch listened to 'Love & Luxury' he would have most likely laughed too. Davis took on drum duties on this one, again displaying simple textures, but as the song progresses, its musical simplicity makes the listener forget what the song is actually about – therefore disposing of its meaning and motive, which might be for the best anyway. Not a career highlight.

'Innocent Bystander' (Korn)

Bringing back the downtuned guitars in order to create the heaviest song on the album, 'Innocent Bystander' is perceived to be linked to Davis' sobriety, taking on the role of what the song title suggests while those around him continue further down the rabbit hole. A strong chorus explodes out of nowhere, Brooks Wackerman's drumming is some of the most effective of all his performances, while a tense bridge has a lot going on – most notably a screeching guitar solo. Urgent, fractious and one of *Untitled's* standout songs.

'Killing' (Korn)

A meaty and frenetic opening sets the tone for another solid album track which shows Korn still have plenty left in the tank. A heavy industrial drum beat hammers along over one of Shaffer's best guitar displays since he became the band's solo player, as more bouts of electronics are thrown all over the place. 'With any kind of relationship or us as human beings in general, we like to take abuse', Davis told *Starry Magazine* in 2007, when opening up about 'Killing'. His deathly growls make a return with even more bludgeoning and regurgitating power than ever before, making this a sharp and to the point song, which is another valuable addition to the track list.

'Hushabye' (Korn)

A twisted love story much like *Romeo and Juliet* sees Korn test new waters with this overly dramatic song. Tender verses feature even more tender vocals and guitar tones, as Davis hints at trying to get his lover to take part in a double suicide. 'You say you'd love to, but you've lots left to do, almost decided to stay cause of you' is an alarming line of desperation, and his anger rises at a stalled attempt of seeing through his plan on a rasping chorus where Arvizu's classic bass sound makes a guest appearance. A mishmash of styles are tried and tested on this highly experimental track, which also brings a certain Tom Jones song to mind with the chorus cry of 'My, my, my, hushabye'.

'I Will Protect You' (Korn)

Saving them until the last song on the album, Davis dusts off his bagpipes for a brief appearance in the opening moments, before eastern music, which the singer used during the writing and recording of his *Queen of the Damned* movie soundtrack also works its way into 'I Will Protect You'. Subtle and catchy keys lead this poetic and morose closer as Davis claims to be 'a ghost of who I used to be yesterday'.

A heavy hook raises the bar and Shaffer fights through the trenches to take a crunching lead at the halfway point, but while still having a strong reliance on electronics, this is perfectly in league with the rest of *Untitled*. 'I Will Protect You' isn't the kind of Korn closer you would expect, but it is a good indication of where their creative heads were at in 2006 and 2007, as they continued to keep evolving regardless of the reactions they would raise in doing so.

'Sing Sorrow' (Korn)

A bonus track on the deluxe edition of *Untitled*, 'Sing Sorrow' is an anthem for anyone who has ever felt sorrow in their lives. Korn's battle cry for fans to stick with them through their toughest period, Davis pulls everyone together with the call to arms chorus line of 'Does anybody know about love? Does anybody care about God? If you're with me, sing sorrow'.

Guitar-driven verses question why this song failed to make the cut, because the riffing is arguably some of Shaffer's best work throughout the whole album sessions, but a relatively safe chorus does put a dampener on proceedings. Ending with a tiny piano riff, 'Sing Sorrow' is a worthy addition to the deluxe edition. An alternate version is also available to hear online under the title 'Once Upon a Time', which includes a different set of lyrics to those on 'Sing Sorrow'.

'Overture or Obituary' (Korn)

A gloomy and proggy iTunes bonus track finds Davis contemplating Korn's future, which perhaps seemed a little uncertain after losing two of their core members in the space of two years. Fearing *Untitled* was going to prove divisive amongst fans (he wasn't wrong), Davis lets his feelings known with the stark line of 'I'm waiting to watch it, I'm waiting to see, is this my overture or obituary?' Musically this is a decent finale where distorted guitars and a lively drum stomp offer hope, but vocally it is a rather flat performance with one of the least emotional displays Davis has put to tape in his whole career.

'Haze' (Korn)

Written and recorded for the Ubisoft video game of the same name, 'Haze' was featured on the enhanced edition of *Untitled,* which was later released in Australia. A heavily distorted affair that includes some experimental and stuttering drum work and vicious backing vocals, this is an industrially charged non-traditional Korn song that just about serves its original purpose. Released as a digital single on 22 April 2008, 'Haze' rounded off the *Untitled* era in less than spectacular fashion.

A music video was released for 'Haze', via YouTube and the Playstation Network, featuring live performances integrated with gameplay footage of that which Korn were set out to promote.

Korn III: Remember Who You Are (2010)

Personnel:
Jonathan Davis: vocals, bagpipes
James 'Munky' Shaffer: guitar
Reginald 'Fieldy' Arvizu: bass guitar
Ray Luzier: drums
Record label: Roadrunner
Recorded at: Korn Studios, Hollywood, California, USA, April-November 2009
Produced by: Ross Robinson
Release date: 13 July 2010
Highest chart positions: US: 2, UK: 23
Running time: 44:40

At the end of the *Untitled* cycle, Korn entered a ten-month hiatus which allowed the band members to focus on their own side-projects. Regi Arvizu launched his punk-infused alternative rock band, StillWell, and released the debut album, *Dirtbag*, in 2011; James Shaffer's alternative metal outfit, Fear and The Nervous System, started work on a self-titled album which eventually dropped in 2012; and Jonathan Davis reconvened on his solo material with his backing band, the SFA (Simply Fucking Amazings), having already released a live album back in 2007 under the *Alone I Play* title.

Returning as a four-piece after officially welcoming Ray Luzier into the band, having already impressed as a fill-in drummer once Joey Jordison went back to Slipknot, Korn began work on their ninth studio album in the second quarter of 2009. Originally planning on making it a concept album where Davis wanted to revolve his lyrics around five symbols he identified as 'the downfall of man' – organised religion, drugs, power, money and fame – he soon gave up on the idea and Korn elected to return to their metallic roots. Recalling Ross Robinson to produce *Korn III: Remember Who You Are* – with the *III* representing the third album to be produced by the band's old friend – the album was recorded with an analogue 24-track tape machine similar to that used on Korn's debut and *Life Is Peachy* releases. After early material had been conceived in Arvizu's garage, Davis avoided hearing any of the music until it had been recorded, and only then did he set to work on the lyrics. With the insistence of Robinson, almost all of the recording was done in an 8x8 cubicle nicknamed 'The Catbox', which was generally only used for recording guitars.

Bringing back the raw vibe of the 1990s, *Korn III* was more simplistic due to the absence of the multi-layered effects which had been flirted with on recent records. Shaffer used various vintage guitars with echoes, long delays and reverb, even playing some parts by fingerpicking, while Luzier's introduction to Ross Robinson saw his eyes well and truly opened. 'I wanted to strangle the guy', he later admitted in an interview, 'he was punching cymbals, kicking stands, screaming ... it was intense.' Recording his drum parts without a click-track so the band could change tempo as the songs progressed, Luzier earned himself the nickname of 'Mr Octopus', as many of his takes would involve him crossing his arms to reach different drums and cymbals.

Instead of stacking four or five vocal parts as he had on previous albums, Davis only sang one this time, making the emotion in his voice clearer. Just like old times, Robinson was up to his usual antics as he riled up the vocalist in any way possible, and in the aftermath, Davis relapsed into depression and suicidal thoughts followed – to the point where even his own psychiatrist wanted to call Robinson and fight their patient's corner. In a 2018 interview which was included in the 2021 book, *Nu Metal: A Definitive Guide*, Robinson admitted learning a lesson from the *Korn III* sessions:

> My knowing of what Korn is, is completely different to where they are now. I wanted so badly for them to be the band that I knew from the past, and it wasn't fair. The performances are obviously not as authentic like the first two records because my idea and what their ideas were aren't together anymore. My vision of what it was was way off and it was not cool for me to go in there with that expectation, and I learned a lot from that experience.

After the album was finished, Davis didn't speak to Robinson for quite some time due to the emotional trauma he suffered, and although the two eventually patched things up, Davis stated in a 2017 interview that he felt *Korn III* was the band's 'biggest mistake' in regard to the material sounding forced, as well as how he himself was taken to 'a very dark place'.

Having initially funded the album themselves, as well as a tour they named the Escape From The Studio Tour, Korn signed to the renowned Roadrunner Records, who released and distributed *Korn III*. The album's cover art returned to the theme of child abuse, where an older man is sitting in his car and looking at a young girl who is standing by the side of the road. Shot by Joseph Cultice, the image embraced minimalism, and with the poor Bakersfield suburb of Oildale in the background, the *Remember Who You Are* part of the album title contained many meanings. 'It's about remembering where we came from,' said Davis in a 2010 interview. 'The title sums up everything I'm talking about lyrically – people pleasing, stress, guilt, fake people, fixing other people's problems.'

Receiving mixed to positive reviews, some praised Korn for returning to their roots while others claimed the songs were largely underwhelming, but *Korn III* still debuted at 2 on the *Billboard* 200 with first-week sales of around 63,000, and in the UK, it peaked at a respectable 23.

To promote its release, Korn unveiled a spectacular live concert filmed in the middle of some crop circles, under the title *A Concert for Korn III: Remember Who You Are*. Premiering on HDNet two days before the album's release, Korn had already posted some videos which included amateur footage of crop circles and UFOs, and in the second video which identified the location to be Kern County, Korn's logo could also be seen in one of the crop circles. A dazzling performance began at sunset and ended in the dead of night, and the concert would later be released as a bonus DVD, titled *The Encounter*.

'Uber-Time' (Korn)

An intriguing scene-setting intro which you can imagine being used as walk-on music at the beginning of a concert, 'Uber-Time' features Korn's guitar tech, Jim Otell, reading an original transcript from NASA's Lunar Crater Observation and Sensing Satellite Mission, in which they shot the Centaur rocket booster into the moon in an attempt to uncover frozen water on and under the moon's surface. All the while, eerie guitar melodies and drum cymbals can be heard as the band sound like they are warming up to launch into the first song.

'Oildale (Leave Me Alone)' (Korn)

Firing up with Arvizu's steamrolling bass and Shaffer's powerful riff assault, 'Oildale' immediate oozes classic Korn heaviness in a true return to form. Less clean in production, the song has Ross Robinson's signature all over it and one of the band's best choruses in years finds Jonathan Davis hitting his stride from the outset. A pulsating middle section welcomes the first urgent barking from the enigmatic frontman, and Ray Luzier's debut drum performance is impressive as it provides an edge that had been sorely missing since David Silveria's departure.

With the song title referencing a poverty-stricken area of Bakersfield which is surrounded by rich oil fields, Davis spoke of 'Oildale' in a 2010 interview, 'The money doesn't really help the local people and it's tough for local kids to get out of there. I feel blessed that our music busted us out.' In its first week of release to radio, 'Oildale' amassed almost two million audience impressions and when the single officially dropped on 4 May 2010, it tied the record for the most charting songs by a band without ever earning a number 1 on *Billboard*'s Alternative Songs – making it eighteen and the same number as Godsmack had also managed. Regardless, this is an excellent start to *Korn III*.

Ruffling some feathers and once again given a good budget to make a strong music video, 'Oildale' is a fascinating and also all too real portrayal of life in the poverty-stricken town the title takes its name from. Directed by Phil Mucci and first aired on MTV on May 31, 2010, the video portrays a young boy leaving his less than luxurious house while his father is passed out drunk. Taking a bike ride through Oildale, various shots of the local area and its poor conditions show exactly what Korn set out to achieve in the first place with their video idea. The band themselves perform in an oilfield and later in front of the ruins of a burnt house, and there is also a direct reference to the artwork of their 1994 debut, as a young girl is seen sitting on a swing while two men fight in front of her; before the victor appears to abduct her. Like the music returning to its roots, so did the video, showing Korn still had the power to captivate and stun.

'Pop a Pill' (Korn)

Led by a strong riff and mysterious flurries of electronics, Davis' raw and irritable vocals hint at Robinson's bullying in the recording booth, as the frontman talks about the benefits of prescription medication: 'Happiness is seldom found, pop a pill, I'm so damn happy now'. Pacey instrumentation finds the bass driving along the verses, and there is still that back to basics feel to the song, which continues a strong start to a promising-sounding ninth album.

'Fear is a Place to Live' (Korn)

Luzier is allowed to show off his drumming talents with some vibrant sections that kick in right away, as he leads the charge on a song where Davis' vocals are shrouded in spacey effects. A lighter chorus still makes an impact, and while the instrumentation is largely upbeat and catchy, 'Fear is a Place to Live' delves into the unmasking of a narcissistic individual who ends up revealing their true colours at Davis' expense. 'Fake ass people surround me', he says as the inspiration behind the album's subject matter continues to reveal itself, and in its own right, this is another triumphant trip back to Korn's early days.

'Move On' (Korn)

A deliciously bruising riff and thrash-like drumming brings 'Move On' to the party, and with an insistent chorus that sounds a little more polished than the rest, this one wouldn't have been out of place had it been included on *Untouchables*. Feeling the pressure of trying to please everyone, Davis soon lets rip with desperate and resigned screams, sounding more impassioned than he has in quite some time. To some extent, this is a gem of a track and definitely one of the highlights on the record.

'Lead the Parade' (Korn)

Focusing on the terrible thoughts and feelings brought on by depression, 'Lead the Parade' might be lyrically unnerving but musically, it brings back memories of Korn's 1994 debut. Containing the most distorted riff, Shaffer has come up with since 2003 and with frantic and scathing verses made all the more visceral due to Ross Robinson's assistance, 'Lead the Parade' brings a modern touch that stands side by side with Korn's classic era foundations. 'The subconscious pain makes me think 'why do I stay?'' says Davis in heart-wrenching fashion, while a strong chorus and a screeching guitar wail cements the song's instant appeal.

'Let the Guilt Go' (Korn)

Another distorted bout of instrumentation lets Arvizu have free reign on a song that becomes catchier every time you hear it. Radio-friendly and welcoming a tense middle section where Davis talks of how people waste their lives away by not dealing with their pent-up guilt head on, 'Let the Guilt Go' may not have been the best choice of second single to promote *Korn III*, but it did make enough of a statement to be nominated for a 2011 Grammy in the Best Metal Performance category. Had 'Oildale' been nominated then perhaps Korn would have won, but instead, Iron Maiden took the honours with 'El Dorado'.

Another decent video accompanied the song's release as a single, directed by Nathan Cox and featuring an air of the paranormal. Using the setting of Korn's Encounter live performance, early shots show the same crop circles as the band go on to perform 'Let the Guilt Go'. For the side story, a girl and some friends are harassed by a bully in school, and when she is out with them in a car later that day, she sees a bright light in the sky. Getting out to take a better look, she is lifted into the air by the beam of light, and the following day in school, whilst dressed provocatively and catching the eye of the bully, she realises she suddenly has telekinetic powers. Using it to her advantage, she later entices the bully to what appears to be a make-out spot and after he forces himself on her, a blast of light comes from the car and the bully turns to smoke. End of video. Revenge is sweet.

'The Past' (Korn)

A future Korn classic and highly popular amongst fans from the very first listen, 'The Past' brings something different with a slightly proggy opening containing some stunning guitar melodies, before the song explodes into life with a delightful slab of modern metal. Davis is in delicate storytelling mode during some tender verses, but when the epic chorus arrives, he reveals that despite his agony, he has no other choice than to focus on the here and now.

Also in the style of what came on *Untouchables* and possibly even containing hints of Issues, too, 'The Past' features Davis' favourite lyric on *Korn III*. Asked by *Artist Direct* in 2010, he quickly responded with this stellar line, 'One that stands out is 'Love without affection is like hate without the pain. Life is a connection separate from the brain.''

'Never Around' (Korn)

A crunching instrumental instantly brings *Take a Look in the Mirror*-era Korn to mind on 'Never Around'. The chorus batters the senses with unrelenting energy, however it is the attractive guitar effects that stand out as they add atmosphere to the self-revealing verses. Despite a strong and sufficient first half, things go a little crazy from thereon as the bridge section finds Davis laughing like a madman. Some squelchy and melodramatic synth adds to the wackiness; in fact it feels like this was perhaps the moment where Robinson's methods in the studio finally sent Davis over the edge. A minute-long playout welcomes some eerie electronics and docile guitar melodies, which puts the full stop to a very bizarre Korn rager.

'Are You Ready to Live?' (Korn)

Straight out of the *Life Is Peachy* rulebook with downtuned guitars and a frontman at his most vitriolic, 'Are You Ready to Live?' is relentlessly abrasive and hard to believe it wasn't written back in 1996. A progressive and refrained middle section contains the much-revisited screams and anguish of Davis, but in this case, it brings Korn back into 2010 as the sombre line of 'All I do is give, am I wasting my time?' finds Davis constantly struggling with his emotions.

'Holding All These Lies' (Korn)

Much missed on the last handful of releases, a strong Korn closer finally arrives as 'Holding All These Lies' opens with a metallic intro. From the verses to a huge chorus, everything is perfectly layered into a huge wall of sound where tempo changes work well, and Ray Luzier gives his best drum performance on the whole album. Dark and dejected in its feel, the cohesiveness of the quartet is pivotal in making this the song it is, and there is even a little guitar solo which Shaffer delivers in heroic fashion.

An epic ending shatters Davis as he breaks down and sheds tears thanks to Robinson, who secretly brought Davis' partner into the studio so he could sing the song in front of her. 'It's basically a story about destroying someone you love by lying', revealed Davis in an interview when promoting *Korn III*, so perhaps it is no surprise that he didn't talk to his famed record producer for quite some time once the album was finished. A stunning way to end.

'Trapped Underneath the Stairs' (Korn)

A strong contender to have made it onto the standard release, 'Trapped Underneath the Stairs' is the first of two bonus tracks included on the special edition version of *Korn III*. A steady and heavy song with a hook suiting the rest of the album, a ferocious breakdown where Davis mutates into his demonic alter ego is given further clout by instrumentation which overdoses on brash distortion; and at times, this is the beefiest Korn has sounded in years. Considering the standard album was only 45 minutes in length, this song could have and should have also been included.

'People Pleaser' (Korn)

After Jonathan Davis' repeated disdain for being there for others who fail to return the favour, it was no surprise that a song titled 'People Pleaser' was written during the *Korn III* sessions. Letting out his fury with boisterous deliveries, Davis just about overpowers Arvizu's bass clout, while simple but heavy guitar and drum salvos are backed up with some effective synth. A mid-album track at best but still worthy of repeated listens, 'People Pleaser' is the final song on an album that proved that Korn still had some angst and rawness inside of them when the right time came for them to reveal it.

The Path of Totality (2011)

Personnel:
Jonathan Davis: vocals, bagpipes
James 'Munky' Shaffer: guitar
Reginald 'Fieldy' Arvizu: bass guitar
Ray Luzier: drums
Record label: Roadrunner
Recorded at: Korn Studios, Hollywood, California, USA, January-September 2011
Produced by: Jonathan Davis, Sonny Moore, Nik Roos, Martijn van Sonderen, Thijs
de Vlieger, Jeff Abel, John Dadzie, Jonathan Gooch, Jacob Stanczak, Troy Beetles,
Sean Casavant, Adam Glassco, Jim Monti
Release date: 2 December 2011 (UK), 6 December 2011 (US)
Highest chart positions: US: 10, UK: 68
Running time: 37:45

Having scratched an itch by revisiting their roots on *Korn III* and with Ray
Luzier now fully settled in behind the drumkit, Korn outwitted everyone with
The Path of Totality.

Jonathan Davis has never hidden his love of electronic music, in fact, he has
even dabbled in the scene under his JDevil alter ego, but when the Bakersfield
quartet announced their new album was going to be metal-meets-dubstep and
drum and bass, a lot of people struggled to take such a concept seriously. 'I
want to trail-blaze,' said Davis in a 2011 interview, 'I want to do things we're
not supposed to do. We didn't make a dubstep album – we made a Korn
album.'

While much of the album was recorded in the lead singer's home studio, the
vocals were tracked in various hotel rooms and closets in Japan, Korea and the
Philippines during Korn's visit to the Far East. Featuring some of the biggest
names in electronic music – Skrillex, Noisia, Excision, Downlink, 12th Planet,
Flinch, Feed Me, Kill the Noise and Datsik; the artists also lent their hands to
the production process while Davis oversaw everything as the executive, and
Jim Monti contributed to the mixing.

With the album's title in reference to a full solar eclipse, where in order to
witness one you need to be in the exact right place at the exact right time, *The
Path of Totality* was more than apt for the name of Korn's tenth studio release.
'That's how the album came together,' Davis said. 'I think all the producers feel
the same way and I'm not sure it could ever happen again.'

Having initially released the track 'Get Up!' in May of 2011, which at the
time was designed to test the waters, the Skrillex-featured rager earned gold
certification after hitting over 500,000 sales and streams combined, and due
to its success, it convinced Davis to record a whole album of such songs.
Containing a mix of mellow and upbeat numbers, which Davis later declared
were 'Future Metal', the reviews for *The Path of Totality* were polarising, to
say the least. While some critics congratulated the band for daring to take on

such a project, others were less impressed with the results by labelling the songs stereotypical and lacking a metal edge due to the electronic elements drowning out the guitar and bass work. It was always going to be an album for the purists.

Released in the UK on 2 December and four days later in America, the Roadrunner Records-distributed album debuted at ten on the *Billboard* 200 and 6 on the Top Dance/Electronic Albums chart, shifting around 55,000 copies in its first week. On the night of the American release, Korn performed an official release party show at the Hollywood Palladium, which was filmed and later released on DVD in September 2012.

Also, in 2011, Korn was inducted into the *Kerrang!* Hall of Fame, and despite its mixed reaction, *The Path of Totality* was somehow named *Revolver* magazine's album of the year at their 2012 Golden God Awards. Incidentally, Korn was due to perform at the ceremony, but they had to pull out after Davis suffered a knee injury.

To promote the album, Korn embarked on a year-long tour which ran through to December 2012. The first leg of the US run saw Downlink, Datsik and Dope D.O.D. play supporting roles, while the second leg welcomed Kill the Noise and Davis himself, under his JDevil moniker. Rock act, The Dirty Youth, joined Downlink for the European support slots.

'Chaos Lives in Everything' (Korn, Sonny Moore)
The first of three songs to feature Skrillex, it was perhaps a good idea to include dubstep's hottest artist of the time on regular outings. Having originally started out as a rock musician himself, Sonny Moore fronted the US post-hardcore band, From First to Last, before moving over to electronic music in 2008.

For many, 'Chaos Lives in Everything' was people's first introduction to Korn's latest bid of mixing things up, but other than Jonathan Davis' familiar vocal stylings, which include moments of deep growling, the wubs and womps overpower any aspect of rock and heavy metal which lurks somewhere within the layers of the song. 'There's drama everywhere' said Davis when talking about the song, the title self-revealing enough to delve no further, and while Ray Luzier does his best to create an impact with his electronic drum stomp, it could have been anyone behind his kit and it wouldn't have sounded any different.

Largely consisting of a live performance where cameras were strategically placed on both the band members and their equipment, the Joshua Allen-directed music video contains a subplot where a group of young boys attack a vagrant, and then one of the boys pays to get into a seedy booth where a woman is dancing behind a glass screen. Underling that chaos does, in fact, live in everything, the boy then takes hold of a games controller and appears to use it to make a man attack another man, and then a priest beats a cop into submission. This is one of the times where the video is better than the song it is promoting.

'Kill Mercy Within' (Korn, Nick Roos, Martijn van Sonderen, Thijs de Vlieger)

Shaffer's trendy guitar work is allowed to kick off this one, where refined verses led by determined drumming let the rockier elements come to the forefront. Dutch trio, Noisia, show up on 'Kill Mercy Within' but they seem happy to play second fiddle, as they supply sultry synth stabs and breakbeats on a track where drum and bass aren't quite as affluent. Although it is a solid song, it falls short due to a biteless chorus, and Davis revisits his dark past with the line 'There's nothing left but open sores,' but without the passion and commitment that people are used to hearing from him.

'My Wall' (Korn, Jeff Abel)

Davis returns to his frustration of being taken advantage of on a song that continues the album's subdued start. 'Every day I throw up a wall and there's always someone out there in the world to tear it down', he revealed in a 2011 interview, as 'My Wall' saunters along in a mid-paced manner. Excision delivers some heavily distorted synth and there are small moments where guitar flurries fight the electronics to try and come up for air, but already this album feels like a Jonathan Davis solo project instead of a Korn album.

'Narcissistic Cannibal' (Korn, Sonny Moore, Jacob Stanczak)

The first inclination that such a collaboration can work, Skrillex and Kill the Noise let Korn take the lead on a frankly monster number. Arvizu's bass has that classic crunch, Luzier's drumming has life of its own, and Shaffer's heavy riffs are highly effective.

Documenting Davis watching people destroy themselves because of their own narcissism, 'Narcissistic Cannibal' has a scratchy and effect-laden breakdown where gripping swathes of synth and shifting electronics morph one way and another; and the first standout chorus on the album is the belated moment of justification which *The Path of Totality* desperately required four tracks in.

Made available as a free download on Korn's website after Skrillex suggested the song should be given away to fans, Davis was against the idea, to begin with but in an ever-evolving music industry and with the power of the internet, 'Narcissistic Cannibal' quickly went viral and Korn's Facebook following almost doubled in no time. Win win.

Directed by Alex Bulkley of ShadowMachine Films, the music video for 'Narcissistic Cannibal' was filmed at the legendary Roxy Theatre in Los Angeles. Calling on fans to attend the shoot, the first 125 people to arrive at the venue were given free entry. Video shoot or not, seeing Korn perform in such an intimate setting was a rare occurrence, and whether people enjoyed *The Path of Totality* or not, this was an opportunity that some could not afford to miss.

'Illuminati' (Korn, Jeff Abel, Sean Casavant)

Giving off a Nine Inch Nails vibe with Shaffer's moody guitar work, and with a beat and electronics similar to that of Trent Reznor's highly acclaimed track, 'Closer', 'Illuminati' is a steady headbanger which finds Davis delivering an authoritative performance. Lyrically focusing on a one-world government with the scathing line of 'You've built this house of shame', Davis discussed the state of the world later on, 'Everybody looked up at the White House and America and everything, and now I think it's like a house of shame, the worst it's ever been.' A solid album track that continues Korn's newfound momentum, 'Illuminati' certainly has metallic components worthy of its addition, and Excision and Downlink add their skills to give the song further power.

'Burn the Obedient' (Korn, Nick Roos, Martijn van Sonderen, Thijs de Vlieger)

Noisia returns for their second guest spot on a two-and-a-half-minute energy-fuelled frolic. 'Burn the Obedient' contains a catchy chorus which is well received, and Shaffer is allowed to flex his muscles with a strong lead riff, and once again, Noisia is happy to accompany Korn in supplying the atmospheric effects without ever threatening to steal the limelight for themselves.

'Sanctuary' (Korn, Sean Casavant)

Originally titled 'November' and only coming to life when Downlink revived it after it was shelved, 'Sanctuary' is about a place you can run to when something is wrong and you are too scared to face your fears. Heavy distortion makes the early guitar work twist and twang before a swaggering barrage of synth leads the charge. After the positive salvo which came before it, 'Sanctuary' sparks and spits as an electronic track, but the feel of it being a Korn song is quickly lost due to its slow and underwhelming nature. More like a Davis solo song, it is he who ultimately benefits the most.

'Let's Go' (Korn, Nick Roos, Martijn van Sonderen, Thijs de Vlieger)

A hat trick of guest spots sees Noisia return one more time, and like their previous appearances, the Dutch trio let the metal shine through even if their best work comes on 'Let's Go'. Arvizu is on fine form with some explosively audible bass work and punchier drum sections from Luzier help the track stand to attention; however, it still lacks something which continues to see *The Path of Totality* begging for some salvation.

'Get Up!' (Korn, Sonny Moore)

And that salvation comes in the form of 'Get Up!' and the mastery of Skrillex. Ear-splitting womps are perfectly incorporated while Korn hit the nail on the head with a crushing onslaught of instrumentation which actually sounds like Korn. A huge chorus gives fans some hope, haunting verses with a slightly gothic tinge let Davis do what he does best, and it was no surprise that 'Get Up!' earned itself gold certification when it was released as an initial standalone single.

Lyrically, the song is inspired by Davis' hatred of people moaning about the recession which was taking place back in 2011. 'I wish everyone would shut the fuck up and have some fun,' he told *Kerrang!* in an interview. 'Every day I've got to hear about unemployment and people starving.'

Both artists are on top form here, and it is by far the best collaboration on the genre-bending record. Skrillex leads a ferocious dubstep breakdown which sends the listener dizzy, while one final stadium-sized chorus demands everyone to 'Shut the fuck up and get up!'

A Sebastian Paquet/Joshua Allen-directed music video showed Korn performing 'Get Up!' to their fans. Footage switches between the band, their fans, and backstage, and the video was officially released on September 27, 2011. A lyric video was also created for the song, gaining positive traction on YouTube, where it quickly earned over six million views.

'Way Too Far' (Korn, John Dadzie, Adam Glassco)
The nearest thing you will get to a metal/dubstep ballad, 'Way Too Far,' welcomes 12th Planet and Flinch to this bizarre party. A diverse vocal performance from Davis is always a good thing, where moments of death metal growling still sound strange to hear mixed in with smothering electronics. An atmospheric chorus is given added dimension with the use of some moody backing vocals, and despite the album getting close to the end, it seems Korn may finally be hitting their stride because 'Way Too Far' is another strong addition and certainly the only song that comes anywhere close to the quality of 'Get Up!'. This one was even voted into the Loudwire Cage Match Hall of Fame, after website users voted daily for the song over choice cuts from Slash, Demon Hunter, Pennywise, Metallica and Hollywood Undead.

To accompany one of the album's standout songs, Joshua Allen returned to direct a conceptual video where Korn take things too far. Not as outrageous as they may have been a decade or so before, the guys still act as rebels as Shaffer takes a race car onto a track and performs daring burnouts, Arvizu gets his face completely tattooed; and Davis prepares to have fun with an abundance of guns – however, his JDevil alter ego emerges and shoots his innocent counterpart dead. Also playing 'Way Too Far' in a small rehearsal space, this video made for good viewing from the off.

'Bleeding Out' (Korn, Jonathan Gooch)
Inspired after Davis killed a rat with his .22 and watched it bleed out, the album's closing track opens with some piano work before spacey synth and dance music-like flourishes add new textures. Dazzling keys swirl around as Shaffer's heaviest riff on the album kicks in, showing off an extended and highly experimental intro. The piano remains as 'Bleeding Out' progresses, and

Feed Me's work supplying the electronic overload deserves a positive mention, even if the song feels more like a remix instead of an original recording.

Largely fulfilling and containing equal components of Korn's heaviness and the dubstep style they wanted to play around with, even Davis' bagpipes find a way to be included for a short time towards the end.

'Fuels the Comedy' (Korn, Jacob Stanczak)

The first of two bonus tracks as part of the album's special edition release, 'Fuels the Comedy' is a nice change in style which finds Davis providing a rap-tinged delivery full of attitude. Kill the Noise provides some simple stabbing synth and fiery breakbeats, but it is Davis who shines brightest on a track as strong as those which made the original cut.

Interestingly, Davis can be heard using a violet ray at the start of the song. An ancient medical device that was used for electrotherapy in the early 20th century, Davis ended up shooting a two-inch spark off of his own arm while Kill the Noise recorded it, and of course, it was a no brainer to add it into the song.

'Tension' (Korn, Jeff Abel, Troy Beetles, Sean Casavant)

Another bout of spacey keys leads this shapeshifting bonus track, where Korn enter a four-way dance with Excision, Datsik and Downlink. During a morose industrial hook, Davis sounds uncannily like Marilyn Manson, which he has done on a handful of occasions on past releases, as the sinister music provides exactly what the song title suggests. There is even room for some of the frontman's classic scat spurts as he brings his JDevil alter ego to the party, making 'Tension' a very interesting listen. The most experimental song on the whole of *The Path of Totality*, it is perhaps a little too out there to have made the original release.

The Paradigm Shift (2013)

Personnel:
Jonathan Davis: vocals, keyboards
Brian 'Head' Welch: guitar
James 'Munky' Shaffer: guitar
Reginald 'Fieldy' Arvizu: bass guitar
Ray Luzier: drums
Record label: Prospect Park, Caroline, Universal
Recorded at: NRG Studios, Los Angeles, California, Buck Owens' Studios,
Bakersfield, California, USA, October 2012-May 2013
Produced by: Don Gilmore
Release date: 7 October 2013
Highest chart position: US: 8
Running time: 42:54

On 5 May 2012, Korn treated fans to a spectacular set at the Carolina Rebellion festival. Including some rare treats such as 'Divine' and 'Good God', as well as four songs from *The Path of Totality* plus a handful of greatest hits, it was left to the final song of the night where the magic truly transpired. While those in attendance were sure 'Blind' would be Korn's encore finale, what wasn't expected was the emergence of Brian 'Head' Welch, who took to the stage with his guitar in hand and fired up the legendary opening riff of 'Blind'. Having patched things up with his former bandmates, Welch officially returned to Korn a year later and he performed with the band at European festival shows in the summer. 'It was after I joined them (Korn) onstage at *Carolina Rebellion*, and I saw everybody get so emotional,' said Welch when asked by *Metal Hammer* about when he realised he wanted to re-join the band. 'The fans, Jonathan, me, my daughter. My dad, the next day, told me he had tears in his eyes. I just mentioned that God is love, and I felt that love.'

Due to Welch now making Korn a five-piece once again, the band's eleventh album, *The Paradigm Shift*, was arguably their most anticipated album since *Untouchables*, and work on the album got underway in October 2012. While Welch, Shaffer, Arvizu and Luzier laid their parts down, Jonathan Davis was going through another tough time in his personal life. Having come off his meds which he took to deal with his depression, the frontman entered rehab to get himself properly fixed, and then his son, Zeppelin, was diagnosed with Type 1 Diabetes. It wouldn't be until March 2013 that Davis would finally enter the studio, and when he did, he stayed there for almost four months straight.

Recorded in Davis' home studio as well as in Studio A of NRG Studios in Los Angeles, Korn teamed up with Don Gilmore – the famed producer who worked on Pearl Jam's explosive debut album, *Ten*, and Linkin Park's first two albums, *Hybrid Theory* and *Meteora*. Early on, Shaffer stated *The Paradigm Shift* would contain darker elements like those on *Issues*, mixed with the heaviness of *Untouchables*. 'The end product is a really good mix of old Korn mixed with some new elements', said Welch during a 2013 interview with *Rolling Stone*. 'It's got a fresh new Korn 2013 sound.'

Released on 7 October in the UK and a day later in America (via Prospect Park, Caroline, Universal), listeners did find an album that was more aggressive, but it was also a little more melodic. Receiving generally favourable reviews for its substance and creativeness, *The Paradigm Shift* reached 7 and 8 in the respective UK and US album charts, with first-week sales of around 46,000 in America.

'Never Never' was chosen as the lead single, giving people the first taste of Korn's new material when it arrived on August 12, and along with a handful of powerhouse songs, *The Paradigm Shift* ultimately proved to be a cautious return as the band acclimatised to being a quintet once again. In relation to the title, where its cover art – created by Roboto – showed a futuristic edge similar to that of *The Path of Totality*, Shaffer revealed the meaning of *The Paradigm Shift*, 'With 'Head' back in the fold, all of the elements fans have loved since day one are there, but we're interpreting them from a new perspective. It's a bigger, brighter and bolder Korn.' A deluxe version included two additional tracks as well as a DVD documenting Welch's return, and in July 2014, a World Tour Edition was also put out, which included further new songs.

In late 2013, Korn embarked on a co-headline tour with Rob Zombie under the brilliantly named The Night of the Living Dreads Tour before the Bakersfield boys headed over to Australia to perform some dates on the Soundwave Festival. Next, they moved on to Europe, where they took Soulfly along with them as direct support, and from October to December 2014, Korn and Slipknot went out on the road together for the blockbuster Prepare for Hell Tour.

'Prey for Me' (Korn, Don Gilmore)
The instantly recognisable guitar bombardment from Welch and Shaffer reminds fans of what they have been missing since 2003, as 'Prey for Me' opens proceedings in blistering fashion. Korn continue to incorporate electronics into their sound despite shifting their focus back to guitar-driven heaviness, and while synth also remains integral yet not as overpowering as on the previous record, this is still a fine start. Reflecting on Davis' torment of detoxing from his medication, the chorus line of 'I'm just a shell of what I used to be' stands tall on a meaty but extremely catchy hook. Highlighting the importance of Welch's return, this stirring opener finds Korn revitalised and ready to reclaim former glories.

'Love & Meth' (Korn, Don Gilmore)
Containing a crunching intro with some sinister synth added for good measure, 'Love & Meth' finds Davis continuing to document his struggles in the lead up to entering the studio, his shaky and pained vocals sounding fragile but as good as ever. *Issues*-esque verses make way for another excellent chorus which

sounds like the Korn of old as Davis reintroduces his deathly growls on this beefy number. 'Love & Meth' leaked online almost a month before the album was due to drop, but thankfully it only heightened people's anticipation and expectation for what else was to follow.

Becoming marionettes in the accompanying music video, Giovanni Bucci creates another visually spectacular promo where Korn perform 'Love & Meth' in front of a demented maestro who appears to be infected by some kind of internal curse. Soon, the band members become controlled by puppet strings while the conductor slowly becomes torn apart from whatever is possessing him, which could also allude to the song's meaning and Davis' constant battles with staying clean. Some horror-fuelled stop motion animation is also a good touch, as Korn's videos are clearly returning to the heights of their late 1990s and early 2000s efforts.

'What We Do' (Korn, Don Gilmore)
A harder metallic edge drives along 'What We Do' with energy and dynamism, where Ray Luzier's drumming takes the spotlight. Synth and keys are used in all the right places, although later in the album their additions start to feel like they are there just for the hell of it. The first chorus to fall a little flat, it is a minor negative on another strong song where Davis talks of trying to get through life the best we can, as the line of 'All our lives are dangerous, but we fake our way through' is certainly relatable for most.

'Spike in My Veins' (Korn, Nightwatch, Nik Roos, Martijn van Sonderen, Thijs de Vlieger)
Originally written and recorded with the electronic trio of Noisia, 'Spike in My Veins' was intended to be included on Jonathan Davis' solo album, which he had planned to release under his JDevil moniker, but in the end, it was reworked into a Korn track. Unsurprisingly fitting more with the vibe of *The Path of Totality*, forceful dubstep stomps dominate a chorus that once again lacks some bite. There is more reliance on guitar power, though and a bright riff welcomes the song in, but a further overdose of electronics puts a dampener on this one and many a listener is left feeling the urge to press the skip button.

Despite a rather underwhelming song, the music video for 'Spike in My Veins' was given a hell of a treatment. Primarily focusing on media manipulation and the US government distracting Americans from NSA spying, as well as the US president seemingly taking away freedoms, multiple videos of celebrity outburst and news reports are shown while Korn play the song in front of a wall of TV screens. No one is safe from the band's motives here, as Barack Obama, Vladimir Putin, Kanye West, Miley Cyrus, Justin Bieber, and Toronto mayor, Rob Ford, are shown throughout – some of course with the finger pointed at them, and others being the victims of media witch hunts. Tackling current issues was a smart move as Korn were returning to the public eye, and while the video, directed by David Dinetz, brings back memories of the band's explosive 'Here to Stay' promo, this one is thankfully a little less graphic and shocking.

'Mass Hysteria' (Korn, Don Gilmore)
Featuring those long-missed screeching guitar rhythms and powerful bass and drum combinations, 'Mass Hysteria' ventures into modern hard rock and has 'made-for-radio' written all over it. This isn't quite Korn on full form, but when Davis sings 'The fire is burning in me', he signals that he is getting back to business. A solid chorus proves a triumph, and it wouldn't have been out of place if it had been included on *Untouchables*.

'Paranoid and Aroused' (Korn, Don Gilmore)
Driven by hypnotic bouts of synth and more masterful Luzier drumming, 'Paranoid and Aroused' is another example of a modern-day Korn utilising all of their weaponry to the best of their abilities. Back to their best with a vicious bridge and a swaggering chorus with some deviating dub synth, this song is one of the album's unexpected success stories.

'Never Never' (Korn, Don Gilmore)
Going from being left off *The Paradigm Shift* altogether to becoming the album's lead single, 'Never Never' is certainly one of the most interesting songs of the bunch. 'You go through shit and you get hurt so bad,' said Davis in a 2013 interview when talking about 'Never Never', 'then you think 'It's not worth it anymore'. Being in a relationship is a lot of work.'

A long way away from the sound of the rest of the songs, 'Never Never' was so different that the band wanted to shelve it, and it was only when Ray Luzier wanted to lay some drums down on it that the rest of Korn became interested again. After Davis added his vocals, the decision was made to include it in the final track listing after all.

Containing a commercial sound and letting synth lead over guitars, the track was met with mixed reactions upon its August 2013 release. 'I knew it was going to piss a lot of people off' said Davis, hence why Korn decided to drop it as a single, but despite its pop orientation, the extremely catchy song gave Korn their first number one on *Billboard*'s Mainstream Rock Songs chart.

Around this time, David Silveria was commenting on social media how he would be open to a return to Korn, having seen Welch recently welcomed back into the band. Asking for fans to flood the likes of Twitter to try and make it happen, Jonathan Davis soon responded by saying he would 'Never, never' play with Silveria again, nicely referencing Korn's latest but certainly most unexpected hit.

Introducing their latest album and lead single with an attractive music video, Giovanni Bucci was brought in to direct 'Never Never' and he tackles the old theme of love gone bad through the persistence of time. Battling a witch-like clock keeper who tries to destroy the band members with remnants of a giant clock and its ever-rotating hands, Davis and the rest duck and dive as they continue to perform the song. With the added slow-motion effects and Matrix-like moves to stay alive, Korn fight back by using their instruments as weapons, ultimately prevailing and thus showing that they are overcoming the unwanted sorrows of human relationships.

'Punishment Time' (Korn, Don Gilmore)

A, pardon the pun, punishing lead riff remains effective throughout a song which also contains claustrophobic distortion. 'Final flight, I'm losing my mind' says Davis as he talks about coming off his medication once again, but while certain moments feature some devilish licks, 'Punishment Time' stands out for the inclusion of some fruitful melodies and a light-hearted chorus. A typical album track where consistency is key.

'Lullaby for a Sadist' (Korn, Don Gilmore)

Written during the *Korn III* sessions, 'Lullaby for a Sadist' missed the cut back in 2010 but it managed to find its way into the light three years later. Welcoming acoustic guitars and an abundance of keyboard work, this isn't quite a ballad but more of a middle of the road rocker. Stripped down guitars and softer drum sections allow Davis to deliver a standout vocal performance, and with a theme similar to what was visited on the *Issues* song 'Trash', Davis talks of hurting someone who keeps coming back for more. 'I can't help to smile at your pain, you wanted to play, but I already won', he says, on a song which is an interesting change in direction from what came before it.

'Victimized' (Korn, Don Gilmore)

The standout song of the whole record, 'Victimized' is an unheralded classic in waiting. Dazzling futuristic keyboards accompany a monstrously powerful guitar chug on a stunning opening before spritely verses flow effortlessly into a powerful chorus. Regi Arvizu's bass work even gets a moment in the spotlight, having been languishing under multiple layers throughout, while an epic bridge builds to a barrage of explosive instrumentation and potent growls. A huge statement that wasn't expected so late in the track listing.

'It's All Wrong' (Korn, Don Gilmore)

Welch is on top form as his breathless guitar work on the final track of the standard album release kicks in, while Arvizu provides a heavy bass line and some more spooky synth adds further posture. One of the heaviest songs overall but perhaps not an ideal closer, 'It's All Wrong' feels like it should have featured a little higher up the pecking order as its momentum quickly stalls out.

'Wish I Wasn't Born Today' (Korn, Don Gilmore)
Part of the deluxe release as well as a Japan bonus track, 'Wish I Wasn't Born Today' is a three-minute bruiser where the title shows Davis' feelings without even needing to hear its lyrical content. Bringing Issues-era Korn to mind again and focused more around the band's metal roots, this a good addition that deserved to see the light of day.

'Tell Me What You Want' (Korn, Don Gilmore)
Another song benefitting from the deluxe edition release, 'Tell Me What You Want' is also a short and sharp rager that is lathered in industrial textures. Robust and abrasive, this is worthy of being included on the original release due to its original edge, which quickly brings fellow Nu Metal heroes Static-X, to mind. It might be a simple song, but it is highly effective in its delivery.

'Die Another Day' (Korn, Don Gilmore)
Part of the Japanese deluxe edition, 'Die Another Day' is one hell of a B-side where Ray Luzier gives one of his best drumming performances to date. With classic Korn riffs, effect-laden synth and a standout chorus on top, this song is almost worthy of being a standalone single in its own right. Upon the release of the World Tour Edition, 'Die Another Day' was added to its track list so European and American fans were also able to experience and own this fantastic Korn song.

'Hater' (Korn, Don Gilmore)
Released as a single to promote the World Tour Edition, 'Hater' follows in the same vein as 'Never Never' in terms of being synth orientated and pop-tinged. Somehow it failed to make the original cut, but thankfully, Korn salvaged 'Hater' and turned it into a made-for-radio anthem after Davis and Don Gilmore put the song together and then sent it over to Shaffer and Welch to add their guitar parts. Once the bass and drums were also completed, 'Hater' was released on 19 June 2014 and its fluctuating electronics and stadium-sized chorus endeared itself to many. Reaching five on the Mainstream Rock Tracks chart and also spawning an anti-bullying music video, Davis revealed the meaning behind the song, 'In the world, everyone has haters. Everyone hates on you because you have something they want. It's really the first empowering song I've ever written'. Good things come to those who wait.

To further emphasise the ongoing topic of bullying, Korn asked fans to submit videos talking about their own experiences of bullying, to be included in the David Yarovesky directed music video. With the upsetting and thought-provoking clips chosen, pale figures provide the subplot, who self-harm, reference guns, nooses, and other ways of trying to make their pain stop, and the use of blood pouring over the bright backgrounds makes for a startling and disturbing concept. With the end message of 'Self-harm or suicide is never the answer. Don't let the haters win – Korn.', the band were once again a shining beacon of hope to many who were in such difficult situations, providing love and reassurance like they did back in 1994 and beyond.

'The Game Is Over' (Korn, Don Gilmore)

Guitar-light but given an atmospheric edge from added effects, 'The Game Is Over' was also released on the World Tour Edition, but it was never going to be able to compete with the impact made by 'Hater'. Davis' fuzzy vocal effects cause him to lose some of his natural refrain, as this reserved rocker fills some space but nothing more.

'So Unfair' (Korn)

Inspired by Davis' son's battle with Type 1 Diabetes, 'So Unfair' was written and recorded to raise funds for the Juvenile Diabetes Research Foundation (JDRF), which is dedicated to funding Type 1 Diabetes research. Released in 2014 but entirely separate from *The Paradigm Shift* (even though it was partly written during those album sessions), 'So Unfair' is a heavy and churning song where Davis' upset and anger takes centre stage. 'I can't help, your card's been dealt, your eyes burn me, it's hurting', he says despairingly. A thought-provoking song that does its job in shining a light on the important subject it is raising awareness to.

The Serenity of Suffering (2016)

Personnel:
Jonathan Davis: vocals
Brian 'Head' Welch: guitar
James 'Munky' Shaffer: guitar
Reginald 'Fieldy' Arvizu: bass guitar
Ray Luzier: drums
Record label: Roadrunner
Recorded at: Rock Falcon Studio, Nashville, Tennessee, Buck Owens' Studios, Bakersfield, California, Steakhouse Studio, North Hollywood, California, USA, late 2015-early 2016
Recorded by: Nick Raskulinecz
Release date: 21 October 2016
Highest chart positions: US: 4, UK: 9
Running time: 40:34

I came back, and I learned that I've got to be passionate about something if I'm going to do it. It was cool that Jonathan let me and 'Munky' just cast our vision to everybody and record and do what we wanted to do with the guitars. Jonathan had to fall in love with heavy music again because he'd been going in a different direction for so long with electronic music, but we wanted to bring it back hard.
Brian Welch, *Powerplay Rock & Metal Magazine*, 2016

After the safe but accomplished *Paradigm Shift* record, people were hoping Korn would go that extra mile on their next release, and with it, allow Welch to fully express his guitar ingenuity in all its glory; and the band did exactly that.

Since 2003, Korn has threatened a second wind in fits and spurts, but *The Serenity of Suffering* is easily the most consistent album the band has put out since *Untouchables*, all the way back in 2002. Somewhat of a selection box of their most defining moments but given a healthy stamp of modern approval, it was music to everyone's ears when Welch revealed the album was 'Heavier than anyone's heard us in a long time'.

Work began in 2015 when Welch and Shaffer took the lead and wrote some of their finest guitar pieces, and for production duties, Korn turned to Nick Raskulinecz, whose long list of credits included albums from the Foo Fighters, Alice in Chains and Deftones. Partly taking on the role as a fan, Raskulinecz was able to give Korn valuable pointers in what he felt had been lacking on *The Paradigm Shift*. Along with a multitude of guitar pedals and tweaking tones, Regi Arvizu's bass slapping technique was brought back to full focus, the guitars were given further volume, and Jonathan Davis' growl vocals were welcomed back with open arms. Those were the fundamental elements in helping *The Serenity of Suffering* send Korn back to heavy metal's summit, and while the band continued to dabble with electronics, this time they were subtly included in the songs instead of leading them.

Talking to The Pulse of Radio back in 2016 and asked about the album's title, Davis happily opened up on his torturous relationship with suffering, which somehow makes him feel safe and serene, 'That's where I feel comfortable when I'm down. And I think people who have ever battled depression and stuff like that, it's not enjoyable, but it's that kind of feeling you can relate to.'

Also featuring Christopher 'C-Minus' Rivas, who provides his turntable skills on four of the songs, *The Serenity of Suffering* was released on 21 October 2016, and it went straight to number 4 on the *Billboard* 200. Having already released the stunning 'Rotting in Vain' lead single to whet people's appetites, the album shifted 57,000 copies in its first week and positive reviews also helped steer interested listeners towards record shops and streaming platforms.

Of all the shows to promote the band's twelfth studio album, British fans were left foaming at the mouth when Korn and Limp Bizkit joined forces for a small set of dates at the end of 2016. Bringing back the original Nu Metal movement when both bands were at the top of their game and at the top of the charts, the sell-out shows went down a storm as both bands provided commanding performances every night. Also, while the band were on the road, in 2017, Arvizu had to drop out of Korn's run of shows in South America, and twelve-year-old Tye Trujillo, son of Metallica bassist Robert, was brought in to play. With many surprised at such a young and presumably inexperienced replacement, people didn't need to fear as Tye jumped in and took to the task at hand like a duck to water. Later releasing a fifteen-minute documentary titled *Korn and the Prodigy Son* and narrated by Robert, the clip looks at Tye and the tour, giving further insight into a young man who was destined to be a star from the beginning. During an interview with *NME* at a later date, Shaffer opened up about how Tye got the Korn gig. 'When we found out 'Fieldy' wasn't going to be able to come on this trip with us, he suggested Tye. It's not just some replacement – this is the DNA of Robert Trujillo, one of the greatest bass players on the planet. You can see it – it's crazy how much you see his dad in him.'

Further underlining the album to include a little bit of everything from Korn's previous efforts, the iconic Issues ragdoll also made a return on the vibrant cover art. Created by Ron English, a young child can be seen dragging the ragdoll with its chest split open, as what looks to be a twisted circus is in full flow all around them. Colourful and imaginative, there are certain correlations to be made with the album's title, and it is certainly one of Korn's most vivid cover arts in their whole discography.

'Insane' (Korn)

Although the song came together relatively quickly, 'Insane' was one of the final songs to be written for the album after Nick Raskulinecz urged the band to dig deep and come up with one more track. Thankfully, and at a time when Korn didn't want to write anymore, they still managed to come up with a ballbusting anthem which proved to be the perfect way to kick off *The Serenity of Suffering*.

Thunderous bursts of instrumentation instantly find the quintet returning to their heaviest of roots before Welch and Shaffer intertwine their guitar work in effortless fashion. Due to Raskulinecz's involvement, Arvizu's bass work is rightfully given higher importance, the shredding rattles sounding audibly immense, and on a song which Davis uses as therapy to get out his latest issues, he sings and roars and growls with renewed passion. 'The song is another chapter in my crazy life' he told Matt Pinfield in a 2016 interview. 'It's about watching things happen and fall apart around me, and there's nothing I can do about it.'

An upbeat sing-song chorus is convincingly delivered before a monstrous thrash out kicks back in, and with some turntable work from 'C-Minus' further bolstering its standing, 'Insane' is a breathless opener.

Based around the concept of *memento mori* – an artistic or symbolic reminder of the inevitability of death, the music video for 'Insane' focuses on the Victorian tradition of shooting post-mortem pictures of loved ones. Directed by Ryan Valdez, a photographer shoots a dead woman who has been perfectly propped on a sofa, but whenever the flash goes off, the photographer sees the woman screaming, dancing, and very much alive. Using purgatorial interdimensional realities, the photographer later takes his own position on the sofa and takes his own picture, which like the deceased woman, he can see himself performing the same actions as his original subject. Spooky, to say the least, it is perhaps more surprising that Korn did not feature at all in their latest video.

'Rotting in Vain' (Korn)

Continuing what becomes the best opening barrage of songs on a Korn album since the *Follow the Leader* triple header of 'It's On!', 'Freak on a Leash' and 'Got the Life', 'Rotting in Vain' goes above and beyond the statement of 'Insane', as in ushers another instant classic. The lead riff is intense, Ray Luzier's drumming is out of this world, and Davis is so much in the zone that he may well have produced one of his greatest ever vocal performances here. Bouncing verses lead into a melody-tinged chorus of gargantuan proportions, so strong that it stands alongside the likes of 'Freak on a Leash' and 'Here to Stay' as one of Korn's best hooks. Subtle spouts of synth add further depth and Davis' babble/scat vocal returns on a scorching bridge.

The perfect choice of lead single, Davis sat down with *Rolling Stone* magazine to talk about the track in 2016:

It's about being in that black place, being in situations that I don't like in life, be it relationships, or feeling when you're stuck and you're just being abused or you don't like where you're at; and you just sit there and rot.

Despite its depressive meaning, the chaotic atmosphere of 'Rotting in Vain' still reached 4 on *Billboard*'s Mainstream Rock Songs chart, and in 2017 it was nominated for a Best Metal Performance Grammy; however, it would lose out to Megadeth's thrash metal anthem, 'Dystopia'. With otherworldly guitar effects, circular bass lines, immeasurable drum sections and an incredible chorus, 'Rotting in Vain' is up there with Korn's greatest songs and certainly their best in well over a decade.

Enlisting *Sons of Anarchy* actor Tommy Flanagan to star in the accompanying music video, highly acclaimed director Dean Karr took the reins to produce another strong promo, where Flanagan sits in a Sweeney Todd-style abode with a crow and a snake for company. Huffing gas which in turn brings Korn's band members to life, Davis emerges from a bath full of leaves and dust, Shaffer powers through floorboards, Welch breaks through cement, Arvizu wakes up from underneath wood and papers; and Luzier crashes through wooden crates. Performing 'Rotting in Vain' in another part of the dilapidated building, the video switches between Korn and Flanagan with a whole lot of darkness to boot.

'Black is the Soul' (Korn)
The hits just keep on coming as punishingly distorted riffs and atmospheric melodies lead this mid-paced gem. Bringing *Untouchables* to mind with its mournful temperament, a ramped-up bridge sees fractious compositions combine nicely with Davis' scornful growls, but it is the haunting elements that really shine through.

The final single of three released, 'Black Is the Soul' originally had the working title of 'Mary Ellen Thrash', as the song was written on Welch's mother's birthday (her name is Mary Ellen), but mercifully that title didn't hang around for long and it was replaced by something more meaningful and more in keeping with what Korn is all about.

Ryan Valdez directed the song's music video where, special effects apart, this fairly simplistic flick finds Korn performing the song while a faceless woman wades through water and a host of mannequins which are falling apart, piece by piece. In the end, the body parts fly around as if they are caught up in a tornado before finally coming together to reform the woman's face.

'The Hating' (Korn)
Not to be confused with the *Untouchables* album track, 'Hating', 'The Hating' is a whole other monster that actually opens with a more refined approach. After a burst of energetic and metallic vehemence, Davis provides a diverse vocal display where at certain points, he includes some rap flows. Sonic pace changes continue this exhilarating listening experience, and the track ends with some vein splitting screams and an obliterating drum section.

'A Different World' (Korn)
When the first details regarding *The Serenity of Suffering* were announced, one of the most exciting and intriguing points surrounded the inclusion of a long-awaited guest spot from Slipknot and Stone Sour frontman Corey Taylor. With

'A Different World' completed and a wide-open spot on its bridge, Raskulinecz called Taylor, having previously worked with him on Stone Sour's *Audio Secrecy* album in 2010, and after laying down his pipes in next to no time, fans were eager to hear the finished product.

In truth, though, Taylor's appearance feels rather underwhelming, his short cameo coming later in the song and failing to bring anything other than extra clout when the high point has already arisen. While the song itself is littered with sumptuous guitar textures, which are proactive against the overall sombre and dark feel, 'A Different World' is the first moment of let down on album number twelve. A good track in its own right, perhaps thwarted by the incredible quartet of numbers to come before it.

Using stop-motion animation made popular by Tool during the 1990s, Korn hired Luis Tellez to create the music video for 'A Different World'. Unsettling and disturbing, the video opens with a man sitting in a rocking chair as he stares at a pipe in the corner of the room, before he is drawn into a bizarre world and given armour in the shape of a shell with wheels. Riding through a building and finding monstrous beings behind various doors, he is guided by a light that is soon destroyed by a large and unsavoury figure. Attacking the colossus and destroying the building in the aftermath, the video most definitely depicted a different world, even if the synopsis was totally out there and hard to fathom.

'Take Me' (Korn)

Another song previously written by Davis for a solo album which instead got re-written and reworked into a Korn song, 'Take Me', is an interesting look at addiction from the perspective of the substance itself. Inspired by Brad Paisley's country song, 'Alcohol', Davis talks of how the drug is not to blame in this case since it is the addict who is the one to come after it; and he used this ploy to address his own struggles with trying to stay clean – having continuously felt the pull since becoming sober.

Led by a hefty guitar drive and dynamic electronics, which add a slightly psychedelic nature to the song's overall theme, 'Take Me' is a strong rocker that contains an upbeat, although lighter chorus. It was the second single released, and considered by some to be the pick of the bunch due to the excellent guitar work laid down by Welch and Shaffer.

Deciding to document Davis' own struggles with addiction, the song's music video finds the frontman in a medical lab, seduced and tied to a chair. Going through withdrawal issues, the rest of Korn perform in separate red cubicles, unable to interact with Davis as a doctor prepares to inject him. 'It's Jonathan's experiences with the substance and we flick back and forth between how the substance abuse and the addiction affects the person,' said Andrew Baird, the video's director. Described by one reviewer as the kind of video from a grunge band of the 1990s, 'Take Me' was a bold and drawing visual, and by the end of the flick, he appears to succeed in overcoming his battle.

'Everything Falls Apart' (Korn)

Focusing on broken relationships in this absorbing number where wistful verses hint at Davis' love for 1980s new wave, stirring melodies make 'Everything Falls Apart' an opulent listen. Even though its chorus is relatively straightforward, it is the evocative aura that makes this one of the standout moments on *The Serenity of Suffering*, while a bludgeoning breakdown switches things up and provides a good balance to the song's unusual pattern. Breathtaking stuff.

'Die Yet Another Night' (Korn)

First, there was 'Die Another Day' on *The Paradigm Shift*, and now 'Die Yet Another Night' finds Korn recycling the song title for another dose of modern Nu Metal. Stuttering verses lead into a brash pre-chorus, and while the main hook itself provides another high point, it is Arvizu who really takes control. Having been given the opportunity to take a more prominent lead thanks to Raskulinecz's vision, the bassist really steps up to create some of the best bass line progressions of his career; and perhaps his best performance on this album comes on 'Die Yet Another Night'.

There were a lot of arrangement changes made to get this song to where Korn wanted it to be, and it is an effort that seems to have been made worthwhile as many fans talked of the track being one of the album's standout moments.

'When You're Not There' (Korn)

Continuous strength in depth sees 'When You're Not There' make its bid for an album highlight. Elevated bouts of synth give off a *Paradigm Shift* vibe as irresistible verses find Davis talking about a lover, and how he receives love is different to how other people get it. A fascinating chorus and further splatterings of synth add a pop tinge to events, while the skies do darken at certain points to allow Korn's heaviness to force its way into play.

'Next in Line' (Korn)

Some fine turntable swagger from 'C-Minus' incorporates further nu metal elements of old and along with a heavy guitar chug, *Rolling Stone* likened 'Next in Line' to 'Make Me Bad' from the 1999 album, *Issues*. From ragged and frenetic verses comes a lighter chorus, however, the death growls of Davis predictably return further in, as a formula Korn do well makes such an attack worth revisiting time and time again.

'Please Come for Me' (Korn)

Downtuned guitars and low-end bass quickly present themselves on a three-minute stomp which officially closes the album. With an intro that sounds uncannily similar to 'Thoughtless', further darkened lyrical aspects find Davis revealing the devil is waiting for him, and when you consider he initially hated 'Please Come for Me' when the rest of the band presented the song to him, he puts a lot of effort into a song which took much convincing for him to lay his vocals down on.

Heavy enough to enjoy but quickly establishing itself as one of the weaker tracks on the album, giving it the job of rounding off *The Serenity of Suffering* provides a rare negative on an overly positive and triumphant twelfth release.

'Baby' (Korn)

With a 'Freak on a Leash' vibe courtesy of some screeching and unsettling guitar tones, 'Baby' is the first of two tracks exclusively released on the album's deluxe edition. A thumping riff and some of Luzier's best drumming welcomes the song in, and as well as being packed with melody as well as delicate harmonies, there is still a moodiness to the atmosphere as the theme of broken relationships once again rears its head.

With a similar formula to the rest of the cycle's songs in terms of a verse, chorus, verse, chorus, mighty bridge, chorus concoction, a phenomenal hook underlines 'Baby' to not just be a good bonus track, but one of the best songs written out of all those created for *The Serenity of Suffering*.

'Calling Me Too Soon' (Korn)

Steeped in distortion and again revisiting the era of *Untouchables*, 'Calling Me Too Soon' features more career-defining drumming from Luzier and further formidable bass-slapping bouts from Arvizu. Jonathan Davis goes into schizo mode on a resounding bridge, and the latest chorus of high quality provides a triumphant punch. Moving away from their downtuned guitar preference but still relying on a whiplash breakdown, it remains staggering that Korn continue to create song after song of sheer brilliance so late in the day.

'Out of You' (Korn)

Annoyingly only released as part of the album's Japan edition, 'Out of You' is the final song from the *Serenity* sessions, and it is another imperative listen. With electronics building tension and another masterclass in songwriting and musicianship, even a renounced Korn manages to produce another song with hit potential. 'I can't escape you, wish I could break these chains' says Davis on a polished hook, and when you consider this wasn't even considered for the deluxe release, 'Out of You' is another powerhouse anthem that rounds off a rather stunning set of modern metal songs.

The Nothing (2019)

Personnel:
Jonathan Davis: vocals, bagpipes
Brian 'Head' Welch: guitar
James 'Munky' Shaffer: guitar
Reginald 'Fieldy' Arvizu: bass
Ray Luzier: drums
Record label: Roadrunner, Elektra
Recorded at: Rock Falcon Studio, Nashville, Tennessee, Buck Owens' Studios, Bakersfield, California, USA, Late 2018-early 2019
Produced by: Nick Raskulinecz
Release date: 13 September 2019
Highest chart positions: US: 8, UK: 9
Running time: 44:20

The Nothing is a journey of redemption and determination, a perennial urge to carry on through the worst pain imaginable.
Kerrang!

Known throughout his career for writing dark and uncensored lyrics born out of the most depressive and horrific life experiences imaginable, Jonathan Davis had new despair to draw upon for Korn's thirteenth studio album, when he lost two of the closest women in his life. While his mother's passing was bad enough, Davis hasn't gone into much detail on that compared to the death of his estranged wife, Deven, whose accidental overdose in a Bakersfield hotel in 2018 would go on to create the nucleus of *The Nothing*. Having struggled with her mental health, as well as addiction over the previous decade, the grief Davis found himself immersed in was poured into the album's writing and recording, acting as a form of personal therapy for the frontman who has always used music to overcome his pain. Intent on giving his most heartfelt performances in tribute to Deven and his mother, Davis spent four months in the studio as he meticulously laid down his vocals.

'The new record is really all about the process of grieving,' he told *NME* in 2019. 'There's sad songs, there's angry songs, there's everything I was going through. The emotions I was feeling, things I felt were conspiring to stop us from making the record – it really was the worst year of my life.'

Calling on Nick Raskulinecz for production duties once again, *The Nothing* may not be as heavy as *The Serenity of Suffering*, but it is darker and more cathartic, with a claustrophobic barrage of downtuned guitars and heavy artillery bass rounded off with a bleak electronic sheen. Even with such grief-stricken content, however, Korn still managed to create frequent moments of buoyant musicianship, as proven on the glut of catchy choruses where melody is key. With the help of guest songwriters such as Lauren Christy from The Matrix and Billy Corgan of Smashing Pumpkins fame, *The Nothing* was released on 13 September 2019 to critical acclaim. Certainly the band's best overall effort since 2002 album, *Untouchables*, it has even been mentioned in Korn's top three albums of all time, and with first-week sales of 33,000, 29,000 of which were physical copies, *The Nothing* went straight in at eight on the *Billboard* 200, and 9 in the UK.

The album's title was taken from a villainous character in *The NeverEnding Story*, and its cover art was created by Nate Rodriguez-Vera. Somewhat open to interpretation, the figure shown entangled in and hanging from wires has been perceived by many to signify personal suffering and how the emotions and struggles faced can wrap themselves around you and tie you down.

On release day, Korn played an invite-only concert where three of the four songs performed from *The Nothing* were done so for the very first time, and while a lot of bands deal with bleak topics in their music, few have ever battled with despair quite as unequivocally and viciously as Bakersfield's favourite sons.

'The End Begins' (Jonathan Davis)
A mournful intro quickly tells you how *The Nothing* is going to take shape, solely written by Jonathan Davis as he evidently remains at odds with himself in the latest chapter of his topsy-turvy life. Bringing in his bagpipes for an immediate appearance, they are joined by sombre atmospherics and drivelling guitar and bass rhythms. With the pensive line of 'Why did you leave?' remaining the focal point, the emotional opening leads to a Davis breakdown not heard on tape in many a year, as his cries of anguish lead to full-on sob-fest before the track's culmination.

'Cold' (Korn, Lauren Christy, Nick Raskulinecz)
Opening up with some stabbing guitars and a ferocious blast of Davis psychobabble and rapid-fire vocals, 'Cold' reintroduces Regi Arvizu's bass click and Welch and Shaffer's down-tuned 7-stringers. Despite the album's overall theme, a positive and melodic chorus emerges from a contorted mass of dissonant chords as this strong opening song does enough to set the scene for what is to come. The second of three singles released, this is Korn deviating from a twisted formula whilst still creating something heavy and memorable.

A Sebastian Paquet-directed music video was also created to coincide with the single release – a live performance of 'Cold' where the character from the album cover dances around the stage and hangs from the ceiling while entangled by the same wires and cables as previously shown.

'You'll Never Find Me' (Korn, William Patrick Corgan, Nick Raskulinecz)
The lead single and released on the day of the album's first announcement, 'You'll Never Find Me', generally follows in the same direction as 'Cold'. Co-written by Smashing Pumpkins brainchild Billy Corgan, Davis later discussed how the song came about: 'He (Corgan) picked up an acoustic guitar and he

started playing the chord progressions while I was singing the melodies. I've never done anything like that before and it was a really cool experience.'

Intelligent and poignant electronics perfectly suit the at times rampant instrumentation on show, where a classic and absolutely scorching middle section plays as if Davis is thinking out loud. His 'I'm not doing fine' lyric unapologetically hits home and again, a strong chorus offers some respite due to its lighter and melodic nature. Continuing the album's early momentum nicely.

Taking a different turn for the videos on *The Nothing*, Korn's first promo from the album found the band performing in a desert after a meteor crash lands. For the conceptual part, the video focuses on experimentation which appears to be on the eve of a biological apocalypse, and while it is a pretty striking watch, it becomes hard to follow at times in regard to the video's true meaning.

'The Darkness Is Revealing' (Korn, Nick Raskulinecz)

The Korn sound of old returns on an unyielding initiation where Arvizu's bass commands the guitars and drums to follow its lead. Sultry tones bringing 'Falling Away from Me' to mind enter in and another radio chorus is gratefully received, even if you are just begging for something a little beefier.

Where 'The Darkness Is Revealing' truly excels, however is in its mammoth bridge, as Davis unleashes a vocal onslaught which includes some fine rapping in a fierce but gallant manner. Droning synth nestles underneath as this track becomes the first real highlight.

'Idiosyncrasy' (Korn, Nick Raskulinecz)

At their most abrasive on a song where the riffing zigs and zags, 'Idiosyncrasy' also fluctuates by presenting wistful verses where Korn dip back into their *Untouchables* origins. A bustling pre-chorus leads nicely into the attractive main event, and with another vibrant bridge where Davis breaks down with the line of 'God is making fun of me', 'Idiosyncrasy' contains all the fundamental elements Korn have frequented over the years while still putting a modern-day stamp on top of it.

'The Seduction of Indulgence' (Jonathan Davis)

An industrial-influenced interlude of sorts once again penned by Davis, 'The Seduction of Indulgence' wouldn't have been out of place had it been one of the stopgaps on *Issues*. Plodding along with eerie electronics and spiky drumming from Ray Luzier, Davis' vocals further dissect his grief with the utmost sincerity.

'Finally Free' (Korn)

Going off-script but adding a further notch to their primitive bow, 'Finally Free' brings another stunning addition to the table. Reflective and solemn but engrossing all the same, this is beautifully crafted through heart-melting synth textures and pop-tinged verses. A perfect vocal performance is backed up by Arvizu's refined but still punchy bass, as Davis bares his soul more on this one than any other on *The Nothing*. A heavier chorus where everything turns sinister for a moment at least, but it is the verses that are a breath-taking surprise.

Seemingly more about Deven than his mother, Davis alludes to her addictions in the desperate line of 'I tried to get through to you, nothing is saving you', before breaking the listener's heart all over again with 'This life betrayed you and you are finally free'.

A music video was later filmed for 'Finally Free' when Korn teamed up with the free-to-play video game, *World of Tanks Blitz*, and they delivered a post-apocalyptic video that may not have been as reflective as the song's subject matter, but it made for good viewing nonetheless.

Helping promote the game's then-newest mode, Burning Games, Korn perform on top of a huge watchtower while the main body of the video follows a man waking up beside a tank and walking through a *Mad Max*-style dystopian warzone. Seemingly the only warrior left he comes under attack, but he is able to find a tank of his own and he decides to fight back. Winning in a survival of the fittest showdown, he is then shown looking at his surroundings engulfed in flames, but having saved the day, the rest of his people return and rejoice in their safety; and if you look closely towards the end of the video, the character from the cover art of *The Nothing* can also be briefly spotted.

'Can You Hear Me' (Korn)

The third official single (released on 6 September), 'Can You Hear Me' opens with some spacy keyboards which go on to combine with some of the heaviest guitar work on the album. Originally written by Davis for a solo project back in 2015, the lyrics took on a whole new meaning in 2018 and so it was reworked into a Korn song. Mid-paced and quickly settling into another stadium-sized anthem, the short and soft verses are shrouded in synth before a spine-tingling chorus cannot be ignored. 'I'm lost and I may never come back again' says a resigned Davis, who laid down twenty layers of vocals on this one, and dipping in and out in three minutes, not one second is wasted on this latest bag of goodies.

The best music video to come from the album arrived as Korn prepared to release 'Can You Hear Me' as a single. Using their own unique way of putting a bleak spin on their chosen subjects, Korn depict toxic self-isolation as a hooded protagonist sits in front of multiple screens littered with social media. Some of the song's lyrics appear on the screen in the form of text messages, while the character also stalks a woman and watches her in bed, in the shower, and out in the real world. Further highlighting how people can become obsessive in their social media usage, the video draws to a close when the woman is cornered in a parking lot and the hooded figure approaches her. Significant and once again relatable in today's society.

'The Ringmaster' (Korn)

Possibly the most straightforward song on the album, 'The Ringmaster', has a brash opening which, due to Raskulinecz's involvement, finds Arvizu's bass taking a crunching lead. Slightly bringing to mind the chugging verses of 'Did My Time' from *Take a Look in the Mirror*, it builds up to one of the standout choruses where melody rules the roost despite its continuously reflective state.

Energetic and high in tempo throughout, it is nicely slotted into the track listing and a sizzling bridge finds Davis adding some beatboxing to good effect. Another three minutes and out song and certainly in the mix to be considered one of the outstanding highlights.

'Gravity of Discomfort' (Korn, Lauren Christy, Nick Raskulinecz)

Harking back to the *Follow the Leader* days, the long-missed tweaking guitar rhythms from Welch and Shaffer make the listener want to party like it is 1998 all over again. Luzier's groove fuelled drumming also sounds like the Korn of old when David Silveria was behind the kit, and together the instrumentation creates a grandiose wall of sound. 'Feel the weight of my pain crushing my heart, it's sure to break', says Davis during another memorable chorus, as Korn continue their quest in delivering a near-perfect record.

'H@rd3r' (Korn, Lauren Christy, Nick Raskulinecz)

Similar in style to what was heard on Issues all the way back in 1999 – from the opening grooves and high note picking to the thunderous drumming and more heroic bass work, 'H@rd3r' is the type of song Korn have produced time and time again over the near thirty years since they first debuted. Davis even sounds like his boisterous younger self with an effortless vocal display, and every drop of Korn nous filters through to make this another go-to moment.

'This Loss' (Korn, John Feldmann, Nick Raskulinecz)

Co-written by Goldfinger vocalist and rhythm guitarist John Feldmann, 'This Loss' takes everything previously heard on *The Nothing* and raises the bar even higher for the final song. A bombardment of distorted riffs and weighty drum sections drive along the early moments before another set of reflective verses are given added tension through screeching electronics and delicate guitar flurries. A moody but forceful chorus is the last of a long list of strong hooks, and an interesting bridge sees Davis add some soulful vocals to a very different bout of Korn refinery. With one more hellacious breakdown where the instrumentation sounds as cohesive as Korn did back in 1994, a breathless number ends in admirable success.

'Surrender to Failure' (Jonathan Davis)

A depressive outro once again created by Davis gives him one last chance to say goodbye to those he has lost, as he longs to be able to see Deven and his mother once again. A teary piano riff saunters along under morbid electronics, and while 'This Loss' would have been the perfect full stop to *The Nothing*, 'Surrender to Failure' is perhaps just as fitting – for Davis especially, as a stunning thirteenth studio album officially comes to a close.

B-sides/Covers/Unreleased Material

'Layla' (Korn)

An unofficial demo recorded from the *Neidermayer's Mind* sessions, 'Layla' features many of the elements which would be heard on Korn's 1994 debut, but its own identity shines through thanks to a wiry main guitar riff and an impressive early vocal performance from Jonathan Davis. The band's talent was evident even on a song that never made the cut, and quite how 'Layla' failed to become anything more than a demo remains quite the mystery.

'This Broken Soul' (Korn)

Another song that failed to make it past the demo stage as Korn worked on their 1994 debut, 'This Broken Soul' contains absorbing darkness through its depressive tone. Sinister but energetic instrumentation further highlights the band's early capabilities, while Davis' fragile vocals delve into the emotional anguish of loneliness and alienation.

Like 'Layla', 'This Broken Soul' is imperative listening and somewhat of an epic Korn track which staggeringly got shelved before the world ever had the chance to hear it, and as good as the self-titled album was upon its release, imagine how much better it could have been with the inclusion of this one somewhere amongst the track listing.

'X-Mas Song' (Korn)

Recorded in 1993 and sometimes also known as 'Christmas Song', Korn's darkly humorous twist on the classic festive jingle features eerie guitar and bass work and Davis' extra emphatic vocals. 'It was the night before Christmas when all through the house, everybody was stoned, even the mouse' is just one of the laughable lines which showed the band's immaturity as their career began to take shape. A frenetic second half goes into hardcore punk mode – something we would never witness from Korn ever again. In 1999, 'X-Mas Song' was included on the KROQ 106.7FM compilation, *Kevin & Bean's Last Christmas*, and that is the only official release the track has ever received.

'Sean Olson' (Korn)

A B-side on the 'Shoots and Ladders' single before appearing on the movie soundtrack for *The Crow: City of Angels* in 1996, 'Sean Olson' is a cryptic and gloomy alt metaller which focuses on child abuse and social rejection – with Davis appearing to alternate between two personalities in order to deliver twisted and unsettling lyrics through the use of some hellish vocals. A mid-paced and bewitching song that has the vibe of the band's 1994 debut, 'Sean Olson' is just one of many incredible B-sides to underline Korn's consistent and quality output throughout the second half of the 1990s.

'Proud' (Korn)

A *Life Is Peachy*-era piercing song which was added to the soundtrack for the 1997 slasher film, *I Know What You Did Last Summer*, 'Proud' raises the roof from the off with a disorientated riff enthusiastically played by Brian Welch. An unsettling chorus delivers where small similarities can be drawn with 'Good God', while Davis' inhumane screams on the song's volatile breakdown, plus David Silveria's drumming masterclass, shows 'Proud' to be a Korn classic in its own right.

'Kick the P.A.' (Korn, Michael Simpson, John King)

This collaboration with the electronic duo, The Dust Brothers, found Korn coming out with an urbanised bopping number which was included on the soundtrack for the 1997 superhero movie, *Spawn*. Led by mysterious synth lines, exciting breakbeats and Korn's already traditionally distorted guitars, 'Kick the P.A.' is a trippy thrill ride made all the more possible by The Dust Brothers, who deserve just as much credit for the creation of this efficient concoction of sounds and textures.

'Camel Song' (Korn)

Written during a heightened period of creativity, 'Camel Song' is one of Korn's most popular non-album tracks, having only ever shown up on the soundtrack for the Arnold Schwarzenegger horror movie, *End of Days*.

Arguably the last track to really cover the band's original sound, 'Camel Song' emerged in 1999 before Korn moved onto their fourth album, *Issues*, which included far more expansive production. As a final swansong to their early beginnings, this huge rampaging number found Middle Eastern-inspired guitar lines accompanying cutthroat bass work and hypnotic drum sections. Retaining a hip-hop bounce but also including some extra dynamics that weren't so familiar with Korn at the time, it is a shame 'Camel Song' didn't receive a greater platform to shout from, as it could have been a hell of a lot bigger than just featuring on an average-at-best horror movie soundtrack.

'Jingle Balls' (James Lord Pierpont)

Recorded during the *Follow the Leader* sessions but becoming a B-side on the 'Falling Away from Me' single and also included on Korn's *All Mixed Up* remix EP from 1999, the quintet take on the classic Christmas song in blistering fashion. Composed by James Lord Pierpont in 1857 and originally titled 'The One Horse Open Sleigh', Will Lyle first recorded what would become 'Jingle Bells' in 1889; however, Korn's 'Jingle Balls' is given a then-modern slant will full-on death metal destruction.

Welch takes on lead vocals on this one, his deep and guttural deliveries making Christmas sound scarier than Halloween, and the song's slow pace makes this sound even more brutal, if that is possible. Not to be played while eating turkey around the family table on 25 December.

'Word Up!' (Larry Blackmon, Tomi Jenkins)

Opening Korn's 2004 *Greatest Hits, Vol. 1* collection, the band decided to cover Cameo's funk/R&B song, having regularly used it during their soundchecks. Also covered by Scottish hard rockers Gun, on their 1994 album, *Swagger*, Korn's rendition of 'Word Up!' is arranged similarly to that of Gun's despite the use of 7-string guitars.

This catchy singalong romp might be more for the dancefloors than mosh pits and Korn don't necessarily put their own stamp on it, but it is enjoyable nonetheless. Ironically, 'Word Up!' became the first Korn song to be sent to Top 40 radio stations and it received airplay on America's largest station, New York's Z-100, which in turn helped the single reach 16 on the Hot Mainstream Rock Tracks chart and 17 on the Modern Rock Tracks chart.

At the time, Korn's music videos were lower-budget and therefore less extravagant as some of their early flicks, and so when Korn needed to create a video for 'Word Up!', they decided to take on Antti Jokinen and put their faces on dogs. Yes, dogs. Roaming the streets day and night and ending up in a strip club, this fun and laughable watch culminates in doggy Davis being pushed between a stripper's breasts while the rest of the band take to the dancefloor.

'Another Brick in the Wall (Parts 1, 2, 3)' (Roger Waters)

The second cover song on Korn's greatest hits compilation, all three parts of Pink Floyd's epic masterpiece were put together to make this seven-minute song a worthwhile listen. Like 'Word Up!', this one does not stray too far from the original, but Jonathan Davis gives his all and Welch's impeccable guitar solo further enhances his talent. The last single to be released by Korn's original line-up, 'Another Brick in the Wall', reached 12 on the Mainstream Rock chart and endeared the band to some new and potentially older audiences, for a short time at least.

'Kidnap the Sandy Claws' (Danny Elfman)

In 2008, a cover album was released containing songs and score music from the 1993 animated Disney film, *The Nightmare Before Christmas*. Repackaged as *Nightmare Revisited*, artists involved in the project included Marilyn Manson, Flyleaf, The All-American Rejects; and Korn – else this entry in the book would be rather pointless.

In a strange way, Jonathan Davis' voice was made for a song such as 'Kidnap the Sandy Claws', as his harmonies, tone and pitch can morph and twist with the best of them. Upbeat and fun, Arvizu's bass contains its familiar crunch, as spooky keys keep the dramatic elements of Danny Elfman's original song. Even though this is a cover, Korn and Davis especially really made this one their own.

'We Care a Lot' (Chuck Mosley, Roddy Bottum, Bill Gould)

Appearing on *Metal Hammer* magazine's *Decades of Destruction* compilation in 2016, Korn took on Faith No More's early anthem, 'We Care a Lot'. Davis is on commanding form with some aggressive vocals, and Arvizu's bass technique was made for a song such as this. Fun and catchy, and again generally following the same fundamentals as the original, this is still an enjoyable listen as Korn pay homage to one of the most innovative and influential bands of the last thirty years.

'The Devil Went Down to Georgia' (Charlie Daniels, Tom Crain, William Joey DiGregorio, Fred Edwards, Charles Hayward, James W. Marshall)
First released back in 1979 by the Charlie Daniels Band, this country-tinged southern rocker tells the story of the devil's failure to gain a young man's soul through a fiddle-playing contest. Featuring hip-hop star Yelawolf, who vocals as the song's lead character, Johnny, while Jonathan Davis assumes the role of the devil, the two square off against one another on a rendition that includes giddying drum sections, sultry guitar rhythms and an overall cleaner southern-less rock sound.

Korn certainly put their own spin on 'The Devil Went Down to Georgia', which they released on 28 August 2020, and while Nickelback also covered the song and released it two weeks before Korn, both versions proved to be tributes to Charlie Daniels, who passed away two months prior.

Further Releases

While the primary focus of this book is on Korn's studio albums and B-sides, the band has also released a handful of other albums over the years.

On 9 May 2006, and after the band had left Epic Records, a *Live & Rare* compilation was released. Containing exactly what the title suggests, the album includes seven tracks from Korn's 2003 performance at New York's legendary CBGB's club, live recordings of 'Another Brick in the Wall (Parts 1, 2, 3)' and Metallica's 'One'; as well as the *Follow the Leader* hidden track, 'Earache My Eye', and 'Proud' – from the *I Know What You Did Last Summer* film soundtrack. Japanese fans had an even better deal when their edition also featured 'Sean Olson' and the 'Got the Life' B-side, 'I Can Remember'.

On 9 December 2006, the then-trio played an *MTV Unplugged* show at MTV Studios in New York's Times Square. With approximately only 50 people in attendance, the intimate concert saw Korn give rare outings to 'Hollow Life', 'Love Song' and 'Throw Me Away', while Evanescence's Amy Lee took to the stage to guest spot on 'Freak on a Leash' – which was released as an official music video to further promote the CD release. British gothic rock royalty The Cure were also invited along, joining Korn to perform 'Make Me Bad' and their own hit, 'In Between Days'. Upon its release in March 2007, *MTV Unplugged* reached nine on the *Billboard* 200 with opening week sales of just over 50,000 copies.

Various best of collections have surfaced over the years, some official and some not, and all generally containing the same sets of songs that made Korn such a household name to begin with. A plethora of remixes have been included on CD singles, most notably during the band's first decade, so perhaps it wasn't a surprise when Jonathan Davis ventured into electronic territory further down the line.

Along with band members guesting on other artists' songs – especially during the nu metal movement when the likes of Limp Bizkit, Sepultura, Orgy and Videodrone were given further exposure due to Jonathan Davis and co being enlisted – Korn as a band have also provided various guest spots. Previously mentioned and in return for showing up on 'Children of the Korn', Ice Cube welcomed Korn onto the song 'Fuck Dying', which appeared on the rapper's 1998 album, *War and Peace Volume 1 (The War Disc)*. A year later, fellow hip-hop artist, Q-Tip, had Korn on his track 'End of Time' – a choice cut on his debut record, *Amplified*; and in 2005, The Notorious B.I.G.'s posthumous album, *Duets: The Final Chapter*, saw Korn feature on 'Wake Up'. In the same year, the Nu Metal godfathers linked up with Xzibit to record a cover of Public Enemy's 'Fight the Power', and it was one of the standout moments on the *XXX: State of the Union* movie soundtrack.

VHS/DVD Releases

Just two weeks before the first-ever DVD was issued, Korn dropped their debut VHS tape on 18 March 1997 in the form of *Who Then Now?* A biographical video which also included the music videos for the singles released from their eponymous debut album (as well as the never-released video for 'Faget'), *Who Then Now?* was certified platinum in 1999 as Korn's popularity reached fever pitch. Re-released on DVD in 2009, the recording was left in its original state and featured no new material.

Released on the same day as their fifth studio album, *Untouchables* (11 June 2002), *Deuce* included the full *Who Then Now?* video as well as behind-the-scenes footage, live performances, interviews and all of Korn's music videos up to and including Issues. Perfect for any Korn fan and still readily available today, *Deuce* went platinum within a month of its unleashing.

Various live DVDs have also been put out, beginning with the simply titled *Live* in November 2002, which showed the band's explosive show at the Hammerstein Ballroom in New York during their *Untouchables* tour. 2006 saw *Live on the Other Side* provide a thrilling set from Korn's *See You on the Other Side* cycle, again recorded at the Hammerstein Ballroom, but despite the album it was promoting, only four songs from it were performed during the show. After playing the 2004 Montreux Jazz Festival, Korn's set was released on DVD some four years later, giving fans a reminder of just how good the original line-up was when they were taking over the world. One of the heaviest acts to ever play the festival in its 50+ year history, other acts to take the stage in 2004 included Alicia Keys, Cheap Trick, Deep Purple, PJ Harvey, Scissor Sisters and Seal. Thrilling the crowd with a greatest hits set and some cuts from their then-latest album, *Take a Look in The Mirror*, Korn powered through the early numbers of 'Right Now' and 'Break Some Off' to cement their performance with punishing renditions of 'Freak on a Leash', 'Dead Bodies Everywhere', 'Faget' and the closing 'Y'all Want a Single'.

Other Projects
Jonathan Davis
The frontman's first venture outside of Korn was to produce the soundtrack for the vampire horror flick *Queen of the Damned* in 2002. In the movie itself, which follows a returning vampire front a popular heavy metal band, Davis' vocals can be heard on five gothic-tinged metal stomps which he penned himself, but due to limitations in his recording contract with Sony, he was unable to sing on the versions featured on the official soundtrack album. Instead, the late Wayne Static of Static-X vocalled on 'Not Meant for Me', the late Chester Bennington of Linkin Park sang on 'System', David Draiman of Disturbed took the lead on 'Forsaken', Orgy's Jay Gordon performed on 'Slept So Long'; and Marilyn Manson laid down his sinister tones on 'Redeemer'. Brian Welch, James Shaffer, Sam Rivers from Limp Bizkit and Terry Bozzio helped record the songs in the studio. Davis would also co-create the soundtrack and score for the 2013 sci-fi/psychological movie, *After the Dark* (also known as *The Philosophers Outside of America*). Working with Nicholas O'Toole, the two created 30 tracks of instrumental and electronic music, which nicely tied into the tension-filled film, where a philosophy teacher challenges his students to choose ten of their friends to take shelter with and reboot the human race – in the event of a nuclear apocalypse. Edgy stuff.

Along with his backing band, the SFA, Davis released the live albums, *Alone I Play* in 2007 and *Live at the Union Chapel* in 2011, and also in 2011, he wrote and recorded a song for the *Silent Hill: Downpour* video game.

Having ventured into electronic music with Korn's 2011 album, *The Path of Totality*, Davis went one step further when he joined forces with Nick Suddarth and Tyler Blue to form Killbot. Fusing dubstep, electro and drum and bass, the trio released an EP in 2012 titled *Sound Surgery*, containing four tracks of which the title track was the most popular.

With dreams of recording a solo album but never fully committing to it, leading to some of his songs ending up being reworked into Korn songs, Davis finally released his own baby in 2018 in the form of *Black Labyrinth*, via Sumerian Records. Introducing some world music influences into hard rock numbers, which also included symphonics and strings, *Black Labyrinth* was critically acclaimed on the back of stunning tracks such as 'What It Is' and 'Basic Needs'; and no one would be surprised if another solo album follows in the years to come.

Over the years, Davis has also provided guest vocals on a whole host of songs with artists from all types of rock, metal, hip-hop and electronica, and below you can see what year they were recorded and where the songs appeared:

'This Town' – Human Waste Project, *E-Lux Demo* (1994)
'Lookaway' – Sepultura, *Roots* (1996)
'Sleepy Hollow' – Deadsy, *Deadsy* (1996)
'Revival'- Orgy, *Candyass* (1998)

111

'Ty Jonathan Down' – Videodrone, *Videodrone* (1999)
'Nobody Like You' – Limp Bizkit, *Significant Other* (1999)
'Take It Back' – Snot, *Strait Up* (2000)
'Year 2000' – Xzibit, *Black and White* OST (2000)
'1stp Klosr' – Linkin Park, *Reanimation* (2002)
'Love on the Rocks' – Performed by Davis himself, *Wonderland* OST (2003)
'Cut Throat' – Marz, *Gorilla Pimpin'* (2004)
'Jerry Bruckheimer' – The Changing, *For Obvious Reasons* (2009)
'Smashing the Opponent'- Infected Mushroom, *Legend of the Black Shawarma* (2009)
'The Enabler' – Chuck Mosley, *Will Rap Over Hard Rock for Food* (2009)
'Witness the Addiction' – Suicide Silence, *The Black Crown* (2011)
'Justice' (Remix), Rev Theory, *Justice* (2011)
'Hear Me Now' – Hollywood Undead, *Remix Credit* (2011)
'Thunder Kiss '65' – JDevil Number of the Beast Remix- Rob Zombie, *Mondo Sex Head*, (2011)
'Evilution' – Datsik and Infected Mushroom, *Vitamin* (2012)
'The Kids Will Have Their Say' – JDevil Catholic Nun Remix- Steve Aoki/Sick Boy, (2012)
'Bug Party' – JDevil Catholic Nun Remix- *Huoratron*, Non-album track (2012)
'Silent So Long' – Emigrate, *Silent So Long* (2014)
'It's Time to Get Weird' – Sunflower Dead, *It's Time to Get Weird* (2015)
'Starting to Turn' – Tech N9ne, *The Storm* (2016)
'Whatever Goes Up' – Bone Thugs, *New Waves* (2017)
'Wake Up' – Islander, Single release (2017)
'Necessary Evil' – Motionless in White, *Graveyard Shift* (2017)
'Jd Fresh' – Fieldy, *Bassically* (2017)
'Gary Heidnik' – SKYND, *Chapter 1* (2018)

Brian 'Head' Welch

After leaving Korn and releasing his *Save Me from Myself* memoir, Welch wrote and recorded a companion album of the same name. Originally having a working title of *It's Time to See Religion Die*, Welch reached out to Regi Arvizu to produce the album; however, he never received any response from his former bandmate. Recorded at Fortitude Studios in Phoenix, Arizona between 2005 and 2007, and containing music with a Christian, spiritual edge to accompany the at times ferocious alternative metal on show, Welch was quick to reveal how entire songs would pour out of him. 'It was as if God was just downloading these songs inside me,' he was quoted as saying.

Initially planned to be released in July 2007, *Save Me from Myself* was finally unleashed fourteen months later. Spawning the lead single, 'Flush', which Welch wrote after accidentally locking himself in his studio one night, the track found him flushing away all the negative aspects of his life in order for him to start afresh. A second single, 'Re-Bel' followed, written after a friend of

Welch's was talking about a child they knew who had been mistreated by their parents. Casting his mind back to when he himself failed to look after his own daughter, Welch used the negativity to create another strong anthem which, like the rest of the album, showcased his impressive vocal displays as well as his instrumental talents.

With other songs talking of drug use, removing the stigma of the 'Sunday Christian' mentality, and the bible, the album received positive reviews due to its overbearing story of redemption. Musically diverse but also close enough to the sound Welch had helped formulate with Korn, *Save Me from Myself* was an honest and powerful release from a musician going it alone for the first time in his career.

Keeping himself busy with further music and literary projects, a clean version of his original book followed in 2008 under the title of *Washed by Blood: Lessons from My Time with Korn and My Journey to Christ*, which catered for a younger audience due to the removal of any profanity and debauched stories. In 2010, he released his next book- *Stronger: Forty Days of Metal and Spirituality*, which included scriptures that helped him on his religious path; and his latest book documents his return to Korn, so if you haven't already given it a read, check out *With My Eyes Wide Open: Miracles and Mistakes on My Way Back to Korn*.

In 2018, the soul-searching and inspirational feature film, *Loud Krazy Love*, received critical acclaim upon its release. Discussing Welch's past troubles and containing never before seen footage of both the positive and negative aspects of his time in Korn, as well as shining a heavy focus on his daughter, Jennea – who has also struggled with her own demons – *Loud Krazy Love* is an emotional watch but also extremely uplifting. Interviews with other members of Korn, as well as Welch's parents also offer an important insight into the man as well as the musician.

Musically, Welch went on to rebrand his solo project under the name of Love and Death, the name chosen due to love and death being the two most significant things we go through in life, and more Christian-influenced heavy metal has since arrived, starting with the 2013 album, *Between Here & Lost*. With Welch on lead vocals and guitar, JR Bareis (guitar), Michael Valentine (bass) and Dan Johnson (drums) rounded out the line-up. Featuring three songs included on a prior EP titled *Chemicals*, of which the title track was a standout, the raw and lyrically honest bunch of songs delved further into pain, suffering, anxiety and depression. Along with 'The Abandoning', 'Meltdown', and a cover of Devo's 'Whip It', the Jasen Rauch-produced long-player was met with near-unanimous critical acclaim.

It took a while for a follow-up but Love and Death returned in 2021 with Rauch replacing Valentine and Isaiah Perez replacing Johnson, and *Perfectly Preserved* was released on February 12. Led by the meaty onslaughts of 'Down', 'The Hunter', and an intriguing rocked up cover of Justin Bieber's 'Let Me Love You', featuring former Flyleaf vocalist Lacey Sturm, Love and

Death's second effort was also met with positive reactions and respect from Welch's peers.

Welch has also appeared on various tracks for guest spots, which you can see below:

'Power Tools for Girls' – Videodrone, *Videodrone* (1999)
'Build a Bridge' – Limp Bizkit, *Results May Vary* (2003)
'A Song for Chi' – Instrumental fundraiser for Chi Cheng (2009)
'The Crossfire Gambit' – Project 86, *Wait for the Siren* (2012)
'A Killer's Confession' – A Killer's Confession, *Unbroken* (2017)
'Masquerade' – Caliban, *Elements* (2018)
'B12' – Grey Daze, *Amends* (2020)

James 'Munky' Shaffer

In 2008, Shaffer formed his side-project, Fear and the Nervous System, which delved into experimental and industrial metal waters. Also including Zac Baird, Elias Mallin (Opiate for the Masses), Steve Krolikowski (The Main Frame) and Tim Kelleher (30 Seconds to Mars), Fear and the Nervous System released their one and only album in 2012; with 'Choking Victim' and 'Chosen Ones' being the standout songs on a solid but less than spectacular self-titled effort.

By this time, Shaffer had also launched his own independent record label, Emotional Syphon Recordings, and as well as using the label to distribute his own band's debut album, the short-lived Monster in the Machine and the now-defunct Droid were also on the roster. Droid were highly thought of by Shaffer, and they were taken along on Korn's 2006 and 2007 runs of their Family Values tour.

Seemingly less active compared to his fellow Korn bandmates, Shaffer's has also laid down guitars on $UICIDEBOY$ and Travis Barker's hip-hop EP, *Live Fast, Die Whenever*, which came out in 2019, and below are a handful of guest spots he has also supplied -

'Don't' – Monster in the Machine, *Butterfly Pinned* (2007)
'Prosthetic' – The Mendenhall Experiment, *The Mendenhall Experiment* (2017)
'Help' – Deadly Apples, Single (2018)

Reginald 'Fieldy' Arvizu

After earning a production credit on Videodrone's self-titled album from 1999, Arvizu's first side-project came in 2002 with the frankly embarrassing album, *Rock'n Roll Gangster*. Under the Fieldy's Dream moniker, the gangsta rap on show was less than well received, despite having Jonathan Davis guest vocal on 'Just for Now' and Tre Hardson from The Pharcyde feature on 'Sugar-Coated'. Unsurprisingly, Arvizu put the project to sleep before any further music was produced, and looking back on the album in 2016, he was brutally honest and embarrassed about what he had created. 'It gets negative reviews from me! I don't like it! But there's nothing I can do about it now. I would never have put it out. I think it's dumb, it's whack, but it's just what I did when I was younger.'

In 2017, a second solo album followed, but it was a million miles away from the monstrosity which came before it. An instrumental album that explored emotion through a bass guitar, *Bassically* included funk, rock and hip-hop across the seventeen tracks. Ray Luzier supplied drums on a handful of songs, Jonathan Davis beatboxed on 'Jd Fresh', and Brian Welch was also brought in to perform guitar on 'I Wuv Bass Mon'.

More commonly and certainly more consistently, Arvizu's other band, StillWell, is a hard and alternative rock group whose line-up is completed by P.O.D. Drummer, Noah 'Wuv' Bernardo and The Arsonists rapper, Q-Unique. Debuting with *Dirtbag* in 2011, the album contained lively classic rock, funk and groove-fuelled guitar attacks. From the raucous opening of 'On & Poppin' to 'You Can't Stop Me' and 'Surrounded by Liars', StillWell offered some promise even if the album's reviews weren't exactly as upbeat. *Raise It Up* followed in 2015 with a greater emphasis on rap rock. Containing a more polished sound which its predecessor severely lacked, the title track and the anthemic 'Comin' Around' found the band settling on some solid ground, and the ballad of 'Mess I Made' was a nice addition also. In September 2020, StillWell's third album *Supernatural Miracle* dropped and picked up where *Raise It Up* left off, as the swagger of 'Gasoline' perfectly demonstrates, and while Arvizu's bass sound isn't as evident, he clearly enjoys moving away from Korn from time to time to create something he can call his own.

Following in the footsteps of Brian Welch, Arvizu has also penned a tell-all memoir, with *Got the Life: My Journey of Addiction, Faith, Recovery, and Korn* – coming out in 2009.

David Silveria

Since leaving Korn, Silveria has used his drumming talents in the experimental rock band, Infinika, which also featured filmmaker and vocalist Riz Story. The band's debut album, *Echoes and Traces* emerged in September 2014, and the songs ranged from acoustic numbers to psychedelic metal; however, Infinika would dissolve less than a year later after an ugly spat between Silveria and Story.

In 2016, Silveria joined the alternative metal band Core10, and despite releasing the single, 'Unforgotten', the group was met with minimal response. Before long, most of the line-up quit and formed Breaking in a Sequence (BIAS), where Silveria and his cohorts have laid some solid foundations for themselves. Releasing their debut EP, *Acronym*, at the start of 2021, BIAS has a promising future on the back of the pounding 'Delusional', and an enjoyable cover of Faith No More's 'Midlife Crisis'.

Ray Luzier

Initially cutting his teeth in David Lee Roth's (Van Halen) band and appearing behind the drums on the 1998 album, *DLR Band*, and 2003's *Diamond Dave*,

Luzier then joined the hard rock supergroup, Army of Anyone. Alongside Richard Patrick (Filter) and Dean and Robert DeLeo (Stone Temple Pilots), Luzier helped the band release their self-titled debut album in 2006, but they would call it quits soon after.

Once fully established as Korn's official drummer, Luzier teamed up with Kings X bassist/vocalist dUg Pinnick and ex-Dokken guitarist George Lynch to form KXM. Having met at a party for Luzier's son, the band name was derived from the member's full-time projects, and to date, the trio has released three studio albums – a self-titled effort in 2014, *Scatterbrain* in 2017 and *Circle of Dolls* in 2019; while Luzier also provided guest drums on the track 'No More Fux', by country rappers Cypress Spring, in 2019.

Woodstock 1999

As with previous events held over the years, Woodstock 1999 attempted to emulate the original 1969 event, which has been regarded as a pivotal moment in music history. With a line-up that included Creedence Clearwater Revival, Janis Joplin, The Who, Jefferson Airplane and Jimi Hendrix, the billing being listed as '3 Days of Peace & Music' provided a defining moment for the counterculture generation, and while 1999 also created its own legend, it was perhaps for all the wrong reasons.

Held at the former Griffiss Air Force Base in Rome, upstate New York, Woodstock 1999 took place over the weekend of 22-25 July and approximately 400,000 people were estimated to have visited the festival across the four days – and it wasn't even a sell-out event. Extensively covered by MTV, who provided live footage via pay-per-view, the festival's co-founder, Michael Lang, later referred to Woodstock as 'MTVStock', as the original founders had next to no control of how the event was run.

Providing an eclectic mix of artists from rock and heavy metal, hip-hop, techno, funk and punk backgrounds, bands such as Korn and Limp Bizkit represented the up-and-coming nu metal movement, while other high-profile acts to hit the multiple stages included Rage Against the Machine, Metallica, Insane Clown Posse, DMX, Sheryl Crow and Jamiroquai.

Determined to avoid gate-crashing, which occurred in previous years, 12-foot plywood and steel fences were erected around the site's perimeters, and 500 New York State Police troopers were enlisted to provide additional security; however, gate-crashing would prove to be the least of their worries. In the middle of summer and with a lack of shelter from the oppressive temperatures which were reaching over 100°F, many festivalgoers complained of having to pay over the top prices for water from vendors. Having brought their own refreshments with them, all liquids were taken off of them when they reached the festival gates, and multiple lawsuits would later be made against Woodstock's promoters claiming dehydration and distress. During Metallica's performance, David DeRosia collapsed in the crowd and later died from hyperthermia brought on by heatstroke, and his mother would also file a lawsuit for negligence – not providing enough fresh water and for event doctors not being able to provide adequate medical care for such large crowds of people.

Violence would become the biggest stain on Woodstock's reputation, though, so much so that MTV would end up removing their entire crew because of how dangerous things became. Setting the tone for things to come, plywood was torn from the walls during Limp Bizkit's performance of their antagonistic anthem, 'Break Stuff', and several sexual assaults were also reported to have taken place during their set. Despite the band's frontman, Fred Durst, calling for fans not to let anyone get hurt, he was later blamed for encouraging the crowd to get angry, but such was Limp Bizkit's upward trajectory at the time, the negative aspects of their set did not slow their climb to global superstardom.

After candles had been distributed by the anti-gun violence organisation PAX, with the intention of holding a vigil during the Red Hot Chili Pepper's performance of 'Under the Bridge' during their Saturday night headline set, fires and bonfires were started with the candles. By the end of the Chili's East Stage show and Megadeth's West Stage slot, the fires had spread and an audio tower was also set alight, resulting in the local fire department being called in to extinguish all that they could. Further fires were started, plywood was torn from the supposedly indestructible security fences, ATMs were tipped over and looted; and trailers full of merchandise and equipment were broken into and burgled. Casting doubt over whether another Woodstock festival could ever be promoted in the future, San Francisco Examiner journalist, Jane Ganahl, would sadly describe Woodstock 1999 as 'The day the music died'.

In July 2021 A film was released as part of the *Music Box* series which premiered on HBO. Titled *Woodstock 99: Peace, Love, and Rage*, the film documented the weekend's chaos through the use of video footage of the bands performing, as well as the violence committed and of men and women walking around the site naked. Musicians including Jonathan Davis were interviewed for the film, giving their first-hand recollections, and along with a host of other nu metal bands in particular, Woodstock's co-creator, Michael Lang, didn't paint himself in a particularly good light when he appeared to blame those specific bands for inciting violence and bringing out the aggression from within many of the culprits. Perhaps even more unbelievably, Lang blamed the female concertgoers for the sexual assaults that occurred, hinting the women brought them on themselves due to walking around wearing very little or no clothing.

Despite such startling negativity, Woodstock's success stories came from the performing artists, with one of the weekend's most triumphant sets coming from Korn. Playing the East Stage on the Friday and with only British rockers, Bush, above them on the bill, Korn was one of the hottest bands on the planet in 1999, having released *Follow the Leader* the year before and going straight to number 1 in America. Opening their set with 'Blind', 'Twist' and 'Chi', an estimated 250,000 people caused frantic mosh pits and relentless crowd surfing as the nu metal kings made Woodstock their own festival. 'Got the life', 'Good God' and 'A.D.I.D.A.S.' followed in explosive fashion, the quintet's cohesiveness all the more incredible considering the personal issues the band members were dealing with behind the scenes. After 'Porno Creep' and 'Shoots and Ladders', Korn debuted an early version of 'Beg for Me', which would feature on their late 1999 album, *Issues*, albeit with different lyrics to those performed at Woodstock. 'Freak on a Leash', 'Falling Away from Me', 'Faget', and the closing 'My Gift to You' ended a pulsating set which left the sweaty and dehydrated crowd out on their feet, but the rapturous applause Korn received upon leaving the stage confirmed their status as heavy metal heroes and the leaders of the new breed to welcome in the new millennium.

   Jonathan Davis still considers Woodstock 1999 to be his favourite show he has ever played with Korn, and it is hard to disagree with that. Thankfully, Korn's full set is available to watch on YouTube at the click of a button, as are many of the other artists from the weekend. A historic but also highly controversial festival that will, for one reason or another, never ever be forgotten.

Monumental

On 24 April 2021, Korn livestreamed a stunning concert, which they titled Monumental. Set on top of a Los Angeles car park – the location of the fictional town of Hawkins in the popular TV show Stranger Things: Drive-Into Experience. Korn borrowed the venue's gigantic LED screen and lighting, and incorporated dramatic visuals and smoke machines to create a show that appeared to be in front tens of thousands of people. The event also offered fans the opportunity of virtual meet-and-greets, as well as various merch bundles. Those taking part in the meet-and-greets were asked to pick some lesser-played songs which they would like to see performed during the Monumental set.

After a creepy opening where the band's unoccupied gear was shown on stage as the intro track from the 2007 *Untitled* album played out, Korn soon arrived, and the show was set to begin, pummelling their way through:

'Victimized'
'Cold'
'Insane'
'Falling Away from Me'
'You'll Never Find Me'
'Thoughtless'
'Coming Undone'
'Throw Me Away'
'Justin'
'Black Is the Soul'
'Freak on a Leash'
'Alone I Break'
'Dirty'
'Can You Hear Me'
'Ball Tongue'
'Narcissistic Cannibal'
'Here to Stay'

With the inclusion of some previously promised surprises ('Dirty' – first time since 2011 - and 'Ball Tongue' – first time since 2015, especially), all who purchased an e-ticket to watch the show were left more than happy with what they saw, as Korn revisited every album from their past by playing at least one track off of them. Performance-wise, every band member was on full form, so much so that the tracks sounded as if they were studio recordings and not live renditions, which is a testament to Korn's continual quest for perfection. Throw in the stunning and picturesque night-time Los Angeles skyline, and Korn had succeeded in delivering a ground-breaking and innovative show that, due to the Coronavirus pandemic which had been taking over the world in the last eighteen months, provided a small period of positivity and entertainment for all who got themselves comfy and logged in.

Korn's Legacy

While the likes of Metallica, Pantera and Faith No More receive universal applause for inspiring bands across various genres of heavy music, Korn is also a band who have influenced many over the years.

For proof, look no further than the endless list of acts that came out in the late 1990s and early 2000s who added themselves to a movement that Korn is widely regarded to have started in the first place. With Korn's flourishing success came the nu metal movement, often considered the last successful era the music industry ever saw before internet piracy ripped the heart out of all that was sacred and holy. While Korn had many imitators who wanted similar fame and accomplishment, as many bands emerged with respect for the godfathers as there were those whose intentions were based more on greed and a lack of original talent.

Pick any nu metal band and they will probably admit that Korn helped inspire them to make shit happen, but there are some who have been more vocal about it than others over the years. Taken on tour by Korn when they were still an unsigned act, Limp Bizkit were able to recognise the rage, groove and hip-hop elements that Korn were able to incorporate into their vicious sound. Just listening to the dirty tone of Limp Bizkit's *Three Dollar Bill, Y'all* debut album, and you can hear the impact which Korn had upon the Jacksonville rap metallers.

Elsewhere in nu metal, Coal Chamber witnessed a young Korn playing around LA in the early days, and they could see the band's star power long before record labels did the same. When Korn's 1994 debut dropped, its impression on heavy music could not be denied, and Coal Chamber would spend most of their debut album attempting to draw off of the guitar textures and grooves that were becoming essential in late 1990s metal.

Along with Disturbed, Nonpoint, Taproot – all of whom point to Korn's debut album for opening the gateway for their own bands forming and earning success, Adema was led by Jonathan Davis' half-brother, Marky Chavez, who had more than a hint of the Davis' snarl in his impassioned vocal deliveries, as well as darkened lyricism to accompany the band's morose alternative metal which was showcased best on their self-titled debut album in 2001.

If it wasn't for Korn, it could be said that Slipknot may not have become the phenomenon they remain today. While the Iowa nine-piece are clearly more abrasive, nihilistic and hate-ridden, their blueprint was taken from Korn as they laid the foundations for the rest to follow. In just a quick playthrough of Slipknot's debut album – produced by Ross Robinson – you find it hard to believe that such chaotic and demonic music could have ever reached the mainstream – in fact, it had no right to, but it did, thanks to Korn.

Sepultura was a thriving thrash/death metal band that took their native Brazil, and then the rest of the world by storm in the early 1990s. With momentum firmly behind them, the band's vocalist, Max Cavalera, became so besotted with Korn's debut album that he longed for Ross Robinson to recreate its sound for Sepultura's 1996 album, *Roots*. In many ways, Cavalera got exactly what he craved, and when he left the band a short time later and formed Soulfly, he would continue to try and repeat the tricks he learned during Roots to give his new band a strong start. Thanks to Korn, Soulfly achieved much in the late 1990s, and they owe a lot to the Bakersfield five for carving their path.

For imitation, look no further than Russian metal band, Flymore, whose 2009 album, *Millennium IV V*, absolutely reeked of Korn. While the songs are strong and create tiny identities of their own, any of the tracks could easily be mistaken for Korn numbers due to the guitars, the tunings, the bass, and the vocals. Outrageous and hard to believe a different band had created such an album, there is undoubtedly respect laid at Korn's door whether Flymore meant to sound so alike or not.

From metalcore and deathcore to hardcore and punk rock, bands containing members who grew up in the nu metal era have also gone on to dabble in the scene, incorporating those same aesthetics into their own music. The likes of Suicide Silence, Of Mice & Men and Emmure have at times moved away from their original sound in favour of creating something more familiar and accessible. Suicide Silence went into Korn mode on their self-titled album in 2017, which was also produced by Ross Robinson. Of Mice & Men took a detour with their 2014 album, *Restoring Force*, and Emmure mixed Korn and Limp Bizkit with their destructive deathcore on 2014s *Eternal Enemies*, and their latest album, *Hindsight*, in 2021.

With a new wave of nu metal also in full flow, as well as a resurgence in original acts who remain productive and creating new music, we have seen Cane Hill, Tetrarch and Tallah emerge and whether they planned to or not, some of their songs clearly follow Korn's formula. Unapologetic but given a modern stamp of approval, Cane Hill's 'Gemini' finds frontman, Elijah Witt, delivering a Davis like swagger on its impressionable chorus, and Tetrarch's 'I'm Not Right' contains an incredible breakdown straight out of 'Here to Stay's rulebook – just two examples of a legacy Korn has created for themselves; and there will be more acts to come out in the future who have also been very much inspired by the band. Is it fair to call Korn a legendary band- It seems so, and there are many people out there who would also agree.

No band in the history of music has had a trouble-free career and perhaps more than most, Korn has had to deal with addiction, tragedy and in-house hostility. Their rise to fame came with many pitfalls, but each band member who fell victim to industry pressures, as well as the temptations that came with it, has been able to come out the other side and live to tell the tale. Brian Welch may have left the band under somewhat of a cloud, but since his return, he has never appeared hungrier and at one with the rock star lifestyle, using faith as a strong weapon in keeping him on the straight and narrow while also helping others face their own demons. Jonathan Davis is perhaps in the best form of his life, still sounding vital and fresh with vocal performances that only he can produce, and Regi Arvizu has also been able to overcome adversity on more than one occasion. At the time of this book going to press, he announced he was taking some time away from Korn to deal with some personal issues, but there is no doubt he will be back on stage with his brothers in arms very soon – where he belongs. As much as their success has provided inspiration, each band member has also become beacons of hope for many, showing that if they can turn their lives around, then so can anyone else, which is perhaps why Korn are so well respected by their fans, peers and industry folk alike.

A band like no other who turned heavy metal on its head in 1994, the genre was never the same again and for that, we thank Korn. Despite a slightly rocky road between 2005 and 2011, they were able to regroup and come back firing on all cylinders to create some of the best material of their whole career, showing that form is temporary, but class is permanent. Korn is forever here to stay.

Bibliography

Books referenced

Brian 'Head' Welch- *Save Me from Myself: How I Found God, Quit Korn, Kicked Drugs, and Lived to Tell My Story* (HarperCollins, 2008; ISBN 9780061431647)

Brian 'Head' Welch- *With My Eyes Wide Open: Miracles and Mistakes on My Way Back to Korn* (Nelson Books, 2016; ISBN 9780718091507)

Fieldy- *Got the Life- My Journey of Addiction, Faith, Recovery, and Korn* (Dey St., 2009; ISBN 9780061662508)

Matt Karpe- *Nu Metal: A Definitive Guide* (Sonicbond Publishing, 2021; ISBN 9781789520637)

Joel McIver- *Nu-Metal: The Next Generation* (Omnibus Press, 2002; ISBN 9780711992092)

Websites referenced

allmusic.com
blabbermouth.net
discogs.com
kerrang.com
korn.fandom.com
loudersound.com
loudwire.com
metalinjection.com
metalsucks.net
nme.com
revolvermag.com
rollingstone.com
songfacts.com
wikipedia.com

Magazines referenced

Kerrang!
Metal Hammer
Powerplay Rock & Metal
Revolver

On Track series

Tori Amos – Lisa Torem 978-1-78952-142-9
Asia – Peter Braidis 978-1-78952-099-6
Barclay James Harvest – Keith and Monica Domone 978-1-78952-067-5
The Beatles – Andrew Wild 978-1-78952-009-5
The Beatles Solo 1969-1980 – Andrew Wild 978-1-78952-030-9
Blue Oyster Cult – Jacob Holm-Lupo 978-1-78952-007-1
Marc Bolan and T.Rex – Peter Gallagher 978-1-78952-124-5
Kate Bush – Bill Thomas 978-1-78952-097-2
Camel – Hamish Kuzminski 978-1-78952-040-8
Caravan – Andy Boot 978-1-78952-127-6
Eric Clapton Solo – Andrew Wild 978-1-78952-141-2
The Clash – Nick Assirati 978-1-78952-077-4
Crosby, Stills and Nash – Andrew Wild 978-1-78952-039-2
The Damned – Morgan Brown 978-1-78952-136-8
Deep Purple and Rainbow 1968-79 – Steve Pilkington 978-1-78952-002-6
Dire Straits – Andrew Wild 978-1-78952-044-6
The Doors – Tony Thompson 978-1-78952-137-5
Dream Theater – Jordan Blum 978-1-78952-050-7
Elvis Costello and The Attractions – Georg Purvis 978-1-78952-129-0
Emerson Lake and Palmer – Mike Goode 978-1-78952-000-2
Fairport Convention – Kevan Furbank 978-1-78952-051-4
Peter Gabriel – Graeme Scarfe 978-1-78952-138-2
Genesis – Stuart MacFarlane 978-1-78952-005-7
Gentle Giant – Gary Steel 978-1-78952-058-3
Gong – Kevan Furbank 978-1-78952-082-8
Hawkwind – Duncan Harris 978-1-78952-052-1
Roy Harper – Opher Goodwin 978-1-78952-130-6
Iron Maiden – Steve Pilkington 978-1-78952-061-3
Jethro Tull – Jordan Blum 978-1-78952-016-3
Elton John in the 1970s – Peter Kearns 978-1-78952-034-7
Gong – Kevan Furbank 978-1-78952-082-8
The Incredible String Band – Tim Moon 978-1-78952-107-8
Iron Maiden – Steve Pilkington 978-1-78952-061-3
Judas Priest – John Tucker 978-1-78952-018-7
Kansas – Kevin Cummings 978-1-78952-057-6
Level 42 – Matt Philips 978-1-78952-102-3
Aimee Mann – Jez Rowden 978-1-78952-036-1
Joni Mitchell – Peter Kearns 978-1-78952-081-1
The Moody Blues – Geoffrey Feakes 978-1-78952-042-2
Mike Oldfield – Ryan Yard 978-1-78952-060-6
Tom Petty – Richard James 978-1-78952-128-3
Queen – Andrew Wild 978-1-78952-003-3
Renaissance – David Detmer 978-1-78952-062-0

The Rolling Stones 1963-80 – Steve Pilkington 978-1-78952-017-0
Steely Dan – Jez Rowden 978-1-78952-043-9
Steve Hackett – Geoffrey Feakes 978-1-78952-098-9
Thin Lizzy – Graeme Stroud 978-1-78952-064-4
Toto – Jacob Holm-Lupo 978-1-78952-019-4
U2 – Eoghan Lyng 978-1-78952-078-1
UFO – Richard James 978-1-78952-073-6
The Who – Geoffrey Feakes 978-1-78952-076-7
Roy Wood and the Move – James R Turner 978-1-78952-008-8
Van Der Graaf Generator – Dan Coffey 978-1-78952-031-6
Yes – Stephen Lambe 978-1-78952-001-9
Frank Zappa 1966 to 1979 – Eric Benac 978-1-78952-033-0
10CC – Peter Kearns 978-1-78952-054-5

Decades Series
Alice Cooper in the 1970s – Chris Sutton 978-1-78952-104-7
Curved Air in the 1970s – Laura Shenton 978-1-78952-069-9
Fleetwood Mac in the 1970s – Andrew Wild 978-1-78952-105-4
Focus in the 1970s – Stephen Lambe 978-1-78952-079-8
Marillion in the 1980s – Nathaniel Webb 978-1-78952-065-1
Pink Floyd In The 1970s – Georg Purvis 978-1-78952-072-9
The Sweet in the 1970s – Darren Johnson 978-1-78952-139-9
Uriah Heep in the 1970s – Steve Pilkington 978-1-78952-103-0

On Screen series
Carry On... – Stephen Lambe 978-1-78952-004-0
David Cronenberg – Patrick Chapman 978-1-78952-071-2
Doctor Who: The David Tennant Years – Jamie Hailstone 978-1-78952-066-8
Monty Python – Steve Pilkington 978-1-78952-047-7
Seinfeld Seasons 1 to 5 – Stephen Lambe 978-1-78952-012-5

Other Books
Babysitting A Band On The Rocks – G.D. Praetorius 978-1-78952-106-1
Derek Taylor: For Your Radioactive Children – Andrew Darlington 978-1-78952-038-5
Iggy and The Stooges On Stage 1967-1974 – Per Nilsen 978-1-78952-101-6
Jon Anderson and the Warriors – the road to Yes – David Watkinson 978-1-78952-059-0
Nu Metal: A Definitive Guide – Matt Karpe 978-1-78952-063-7
Tommy Bolin: In and Out of Deep Purple – Laura Shenton 978-1-78952-070-5
Maximum Darkness – Deke Leonard 978-1-78952-048-4
Maybe I Should've Stayed In Bed – Deke Leonard 978-1-78952-053-8
The Twang Dynasty – Deke Leonard 978-1-78952-049-1

and many more to come!

Would you like to write for Sonicbond Publishing?

We are mainly a music publisher, but we also occasionally publish in other genres including film and television. At Sonicbond Publishing we are always on the look-out for authors, particularly for our two main series, On Track and Decades.

Mixing fact with in depth analysis, the On Track series examines the entire recorded work of a particular musical artist or group. All genres are considered from easy listening and jazz to 60s soul to 90s pop, via rock and metal.

The Decades series singles out a particular decade in an artist or group's history and focuses on that decade in more detail than may be allowed in the On Track series.

While professional writing experience would, of course, be an advantage, the most important qualification is to have real enthusiasm and knowledge of your subject. First-time authors are welcomed, but the ability to write well in English is essential.

Sonicbond Publishing has distribution throughout Europe and North America, and all our books are also published in E-book form. Authors will be paid a royalty based on sales of their book. Further details about our books are available from www.sonicbondpublishing.com. To contact us, complete the contact form there or email info@sonicbondpublishing.co.uk